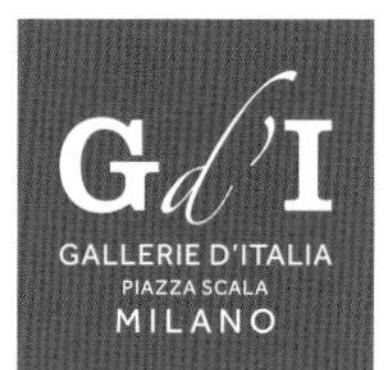
Gd'I
GALLERIE D'ITALIA
PIAZZA SCALA
MILANO

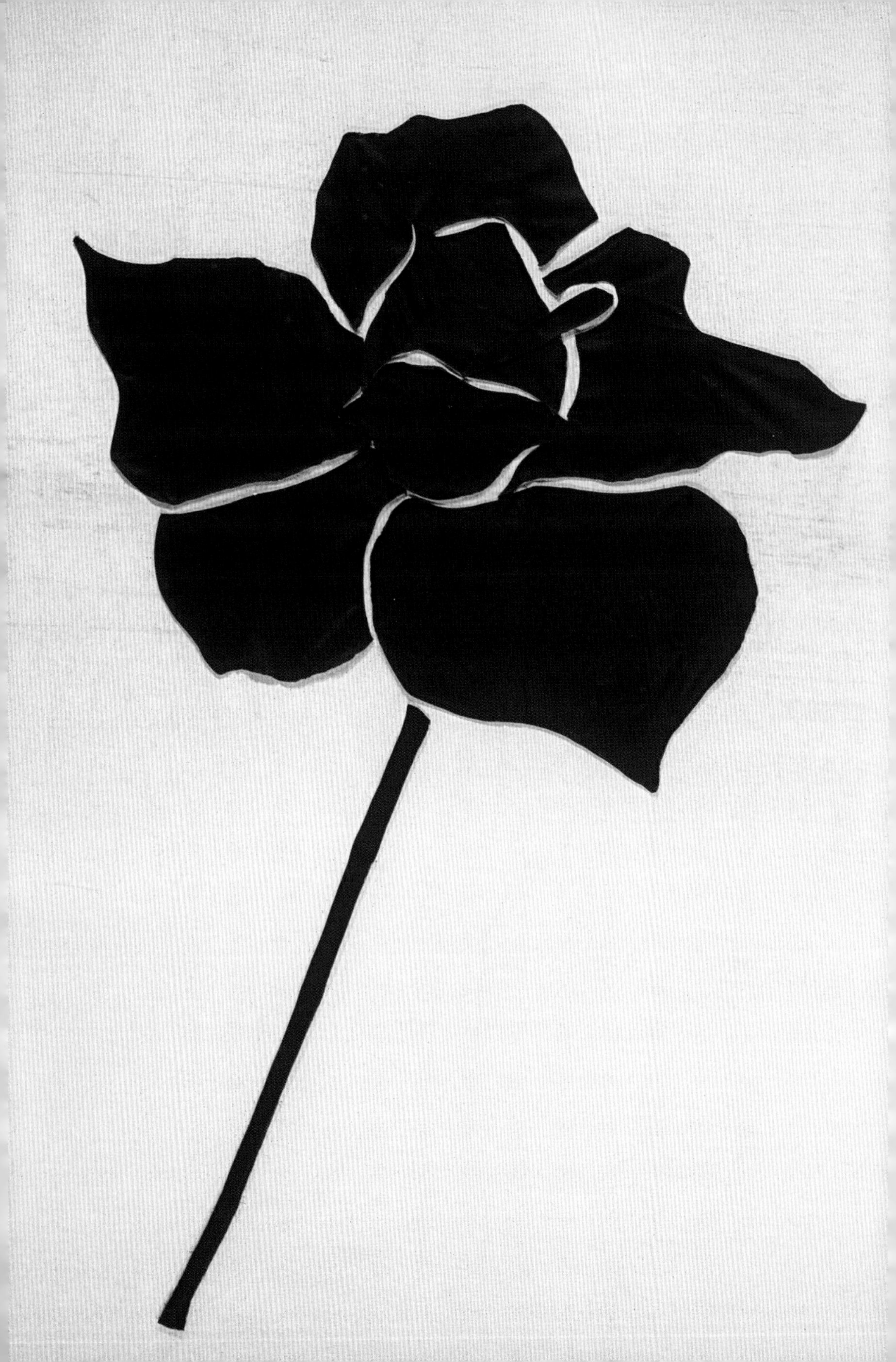

ART AS REVELATION

FROM THE LUIGI AND PEPPINO AGRATI COLLECTION

EDITED BY
LUCA MASSIMO BARBERO

SilvanaEditoriale

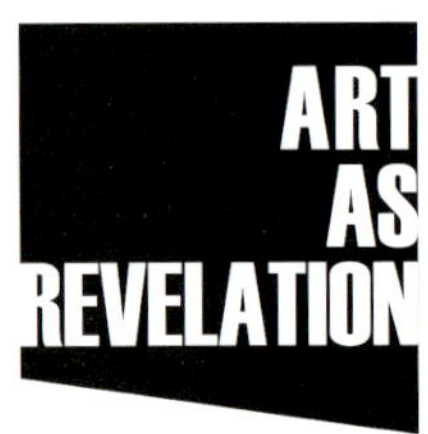

FROM THE
LUIGI AND PEPPINO AGRATI
COLLECTION

Curator
Luca Massimo Barbero

Intesa Sanpaolo

Giovanni Bazoli
Chairman Emeritus

Gian Maria Gros-Pietro
Chairman

Carlo Messina
Managing Director
and Chief Executive Officer

Paolo M. Grandi
Chief Governance Officer

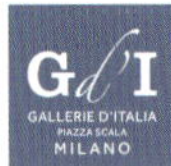

Gallerie d'Italia
Piazza Scala, Milan
16 May – 19 August, 2018

Exhibition project conceived and conducted by

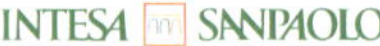

This exhibition is part of
Progetto Cultura

Under the patronage of

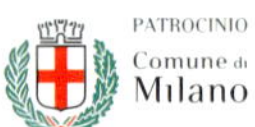

Organisation

Intesa Sanpaolo
Art, Culture and Historical Heritage Head Office Department

Head Officer
Michele Coppola

Historical Artistic Heritage and Cultural Activities
Silvia Foschi

Artistic Heritage
Laura Feliciotti with Massimo Alessandro Bianchi, Isabella Cairoli, Sara Pozzato, Sonia Riello, Alessandro Vanin

Cultural Initiatives and Exhibition Projects
Antonio Ernesto Denunzio with Francesca Dal Cortivo

Historical Archives
Barbara Costa with Serena Berno

Promotion, Marketing and Cultural Partnerships
Laurence Aliquot

Promotion and Cultural Marketing
Marie Évangéline Maillard with Simona Cantone, Gaia Dell'Orto, Andrea Maria Rossetti

Publishing and Music Initiatives Coordination
Rosanna Benedini with Valeria Tortosa

Exhibition Set-up Coordination
Mariangela Taliento

Museum Complex Coordination
Giovanni Morale

Administrative Support
Carlo Serra with Elisabetta Ferrari

Editing
Romina Paola Elia

Special thanks to the divisions of Intesa Sanpaolo Group for their collaboration

Procurement Head Office Department
Administration and Tax Head Office Department
Real Estate and Logistics Head Office Department
Legal Affairs Head Office Department – Group General Counsel
Communication and Corporate Image Head Office Department
Corporate Bodies Secretariats and General Affairs Head Office Department
Internal Communication

Production

Production Coordinator
Gianfranco Brunelli

Scientific Coordinator
Chiara Mari

Layout Design
Valter Palmieri

Lighting Designer
Giovanni Caprotti

Visuals and Graphic Design Project
Nexo

Restoration and Condition Reports for the Works on Display
Studio Restauri Formica – Luciano Formica, Patrizia Buratti and David Formica
Valentina Piovan – Restauro opere d'arte

Multimedia Installations
Zenit Arti Audiovisive

Exhibition Signage Translation
Alphaville. Traduzioni e servizi editoriali

Guided Visits and Educational Workshops
Opera Laboratori Fiorentini

Special thanks to
Minjung Kim, Laura Corazzol, Maria Teresa Panzeri, Achille Galdini, Andrea M. Massari

This exhibition was created to pay homage and celebrate the memory of Cavaliere del Lavoro Luigi Agrati, and was made possible thanks to Mrs Maria Giulia Fumagalli Agrati's generous support.

Art and culture are so ingrained in the history and life of our country that they represent the deepest and truest expression of its identity. So much so that even domains apparently alien to the realm of art, such as businesses, have thoroughly embraced it along with its most enlightened practitioners, producing economic prosperity while at the same time promoting our values and artistic heritage.
Clear evidence of this concept has been provided by the Agrati brothers, who, during the latter part of the twentieth century, created what is today one of the most important private collections of modern art in Italy and the world, thus reconciling their entrepreneurial obligations and their cultural awareness and passion for art.
The Agratis' personal relationships with artists, critics, and gallery owners around the world, and their rare ability to intuit the trends and artists that would later achieve international recognition, gave birth to the Luigi and Peppino Agrati Collection, a corpus of 500 works of Italian, European, and American art of the second half of the twentieth century. With works ranging from Burri, Fontana, Schifano, Melotti, Boetti, and Paolini to Christo, Rauschenberg, Warhol, Lichtenstein, Flavin, LeWitt, Ryman, Twombly, and Basquiat, the collection, whose openness to American artistic innovation is unique in Italy, highlights the richness and complexity of postwar art through works of enormous importance.
With extraordinary generosity, Luigi Agrati, recipient of the Italian Order of Merit

for Labour, entrusted his collection to the Intesa Sanpaolo, with the dual goals of making it known to the members of the community and of displaying it in an appropriate setting. In this way, the artistic heritage of our bank has been enriched by a nucleus of works of inestimable value.
To honor and remember Agrati and renew our thanks to his wife Mariuccia for the friendship and trust she has always shown us, a selection of pieces from the collection is now being presented to the public—a preview of what will be its final form. Hosted by the Gallerie d'Italia, in Piazza Scala, and curated by Luca Massimo Barbero, Art as Revelation *presents 73 masterpieces from the collection: a thrilling encounter that allows visitors to experience some of the most significant works of Italian and American art of the last century. This important exhibition reconstructs the intellectual journey of the brothers who discovered and acquired these works, encapsulating the history of a collection regarded internationally as a paragon of art collecting.*

Giovanni Bazoli
Chairman Emeritus
Intesa Sanpaolo

CONTENTS

CATALOGUE

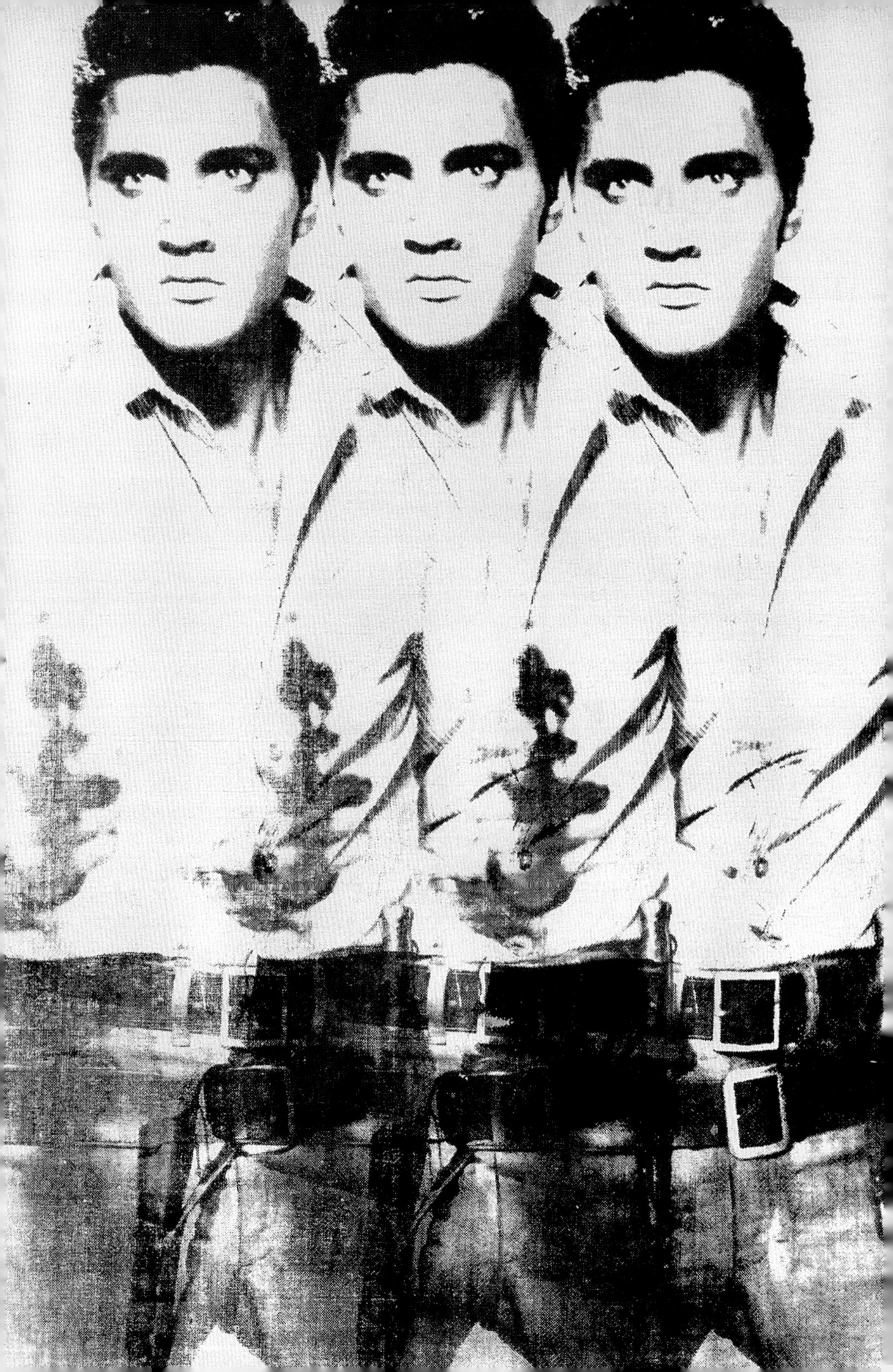

ART AS *REVELATION* OF CONTEMPORARY LIFE

LUCA MASSIMO BARBERO

The collection created by the industrialists Luigi and Peppino Agrati marks a high point in the history of art collecting in Italy during the second half of the twentieth century. Members of the enlightened Lombard bourgeoisie, the Agrati brothers shared remarkable instincts for understanding the depth of the images that shaped their time. Their collection applies 'sharply focused attention to modernity, with a decidedly international outlook, comparable in some ways to the aspirations that have guided [...] a few other Italian collectors looking toward American art, starting with Giorgio Franchetti and Giuseppe Panza di Biumo'.[1]

The collection began to take shape in the 1960s, inspired by Peppino Agrati's passion for art. Together with Luigi, he conceived of collecting as a personal vision, freed from fads and market trends. The two collectors forged close relationships with artists, frequented the most important exhibition spaces, and became involved in debates across the whole spectrum of international art. As a result, the collection, often with great precociousness, welcomed artistic investigations that would be acknowledged only later as watershed moments in the art of the second half of the twentieth century. Furthermore, it allowed for fascinating, fresh interactions between the latest developments in Italian and European art from the 1950s to the 1980s and trends in contemporary international art, with particular attention to currents in American art of the 1960s and 1970s.

In the spirit of both Germano Celant's 2002 monograph[2], the first to trace the history of the collection and the collectors, and the detailed, systematic study of the works of art in Francesco Tedeschi's 2012 catalogue raisonné[3], the present exhibition reveals to the public for the first time a representative selection of pieces, reflecting the broad diversity of the collection, the simultaneous presence of Italian and American culture, and continuing interest in certain artists.

One of the Agratis' most important relationships was with Fausto Melotti, whom, together with Lucio Fontana, the brothers recognised as a radical leader of twentieth-century Italian art. The two artists had already met in Milan in the 1930s, when both of them frequented the lively Galleria Il Milione, and caught up with each other again in the same city in the spring of 1947, when Fontana returned from Argentina. Milan had been devastated by the war, but reconstruction had begun immediately, and a famous photo by Fontana, found in the ruins of his studio, became a symbol of this rebirth. It was in this environment that industries like the Agratis' metal engineering company grew, founded in 1939 on an almost artisanal scale and ready to develop into a huge metalworking enterprise in the 1950s and 60s. It is therefore significant—almost a harking back to their roots—that when the collection was launched, attention was focused not only on the latest experimentation, but on two central figures in the world of 1930s art, whose inexhaustible vitality was fertile ground for exchanges with the first generations of artists of the postwar period.

In the close relationship that Peppino Agrati forged with Fausto Melotti, the collector's intuition was inspired by the artist's extraordinary, clearheaded, wild love affair with art, as seen in the title of his poetic work *Un folle amore* (A Crazy Love) from 1971.

The important nucleus of works in the collection exemplifies the diversity of forms and modes of creative expression during the intense period of artistic activity following the Second World War. While Melotti's sculpture *Savio* recalls abstract work of the 1930s, his four imposing *Korai* are mature examples of his extraordinary interpretation of the techniques of working in ceramics. At the end of the 1950s, Melotti began experimenting with the use of ductile metals like brass, which allowed him to create fragile figures in space in an intensely narrative folktale vein. From *Senza titolo (I giocolieri)* (*Untitled* [*The Jugglers*]), 1959–60, to his works from the early '80s, like *La zingara* (*The Gypsy Woman*) from 1980, his sculptures reflect the new vitality of his artistic language, in which the music of geometry finds new narrative possibilities in a modification of form similar to that of a musical composition.

Although there was a lesser number of pieces by Lucio Fontana in the collection, he is represented by works of great significance, among which is the rare 1957 *Concetto spaziale* (*Spatial Concept*), exhibited in a space devoted to him alone in the Venice Biennale the following year. The choice reveals the Agratis' sensitive appreciation of not only the best-known works but of those that are more subtly evocative as well. Fontana here is liberated from the baroque material that characterised his previous phase and has immersed the canvas with an almost airy hue. It is precisely in some of his *Inchiostri* (*Inks*), the cycle of which the work is part, that the artist extended this technique toward the end of 1958, creating his first '*Tagli*' ('*Cuts*'). This new phase is represented in the collection by *Concetto Spaziale: Attese* (*Spatial Concept: Waiting*), from 1965, a classic, mature example of his work with an intense color palette. From the same year come the '*Teatrini*' ('*Little Theatres*'), as the artist informally called the series of works composed of backdrops and lacquered wooden frames in vibrant colors, which create a kind of theater scenery.[4] In the work acquired by the Agratis, the edges are cut to delineate irregular spheres, similar to those in *Nature* (*Natures*), originally created in terra cotta and later cast in bronze. Exhibited in 1960 in the show entitled *Dalla natura all'arte* (*From Nature to Art*), organized at the Palazzo Grassi in Venice around the idea of Mother Nature, the *Nature* series can be defined as 'cosmic' sculpture, 'solid forms', as the artist wrote, 'created with a desire to make inert material come to life'.[5]

Fontana's vigorous modernity is reflected in that of Milan at the time, a city which, in 1957, hosted one of the most important exhibitions of the latest trends in art at the end of the decade: Yves Klein's one-man show opened in January at the Galleria Apollinaire. The artist, who shortly afterward would sign the Manifesto of Nouveau Réalisme, presented, for the first time in Italy, his blue *'Propositions monochromes'* (*'Monochrome Propositions'*), which, at the time, generated opposing opinions ranging from appreciation to outrage. Fontana, always generous toward the young, and one of the first to purchase their works, understood Klein's intellectual qualities and his poetry of color intended as an ideal, infinite space of pure perception.

Toward the end of the 1950s, Fontana was recognized as the leader of the young artists who were going beyond the subjectivity and material exuberance of *arte informale* (*Informalism*) and moving in the direction of monochromatic painting and an objective, impersonal conception of art. One need only think about Fontana's relationship with Piero Manzoni and Enrico Castellani, who, in 1959, paid homage to him in the first issue of the periodical *Azimuth*.[6] Champions of investigating the possibilities of a monochromatic surface as a limitless, completely free field of expression, Manzoni and Castellani are present in this exhibition with two mature works: a 'hairy' *Achrome* from 1961 and a large diptych from 1967. These works are positioned to engage in a dialogue with one of American artist Robert Ryman's masterpieces acquired by Peppino Agrati: *Winsor 20*, from 1966, in which the field of white becomes a place of 'enlightenment', to use the term coined by the artist himself.

The brand-new adventure with monochromatic painting had, in a sense, a precedent and counterpoint in the only work by Alberto Burri in the collection, *Bianco Rosso* (*White Red*), from 1954. Like Fontana, Burri was also considered a mentor by young Roman artists striking out at the end of the 1950s. He was less interested in the existential subject matter of his paintings than in the almost atonal music of some of his works, such as some of the 'Ferri' (works in steel) at the end of the decade. Originating precisely in the investigation of the surface as a monochromatic 'screen', the laboratory of new Roman figurative painting came into being at the beginning of the 1960s, often superficially labelled as Pop Art.[7] The difference is clearly seen in the works by Mario Schifano and Jannis Kounellis exhibited in this show. In contrast to the American artists who adopted silk screen or an almost mechanical way of painting, related to images from publicity and mass culture, the Italians still insisted on 'handmade' painting. It wasn't by chance that Schifano spoke of 'sign painters', referring to the anonymous artists who painted billboards intended for the new highways and walls of the city. Inspired by his own urban landscape, Kounellis created his graphic alphabet of symbols, shapes, letters, and numbers that stood out against an interplay of black and white, the color palette of the decade, translating the epic dimension of the city and transposing it into a new visual grammar. His next and best-known *'Rose'* (*'Roses'*) are, in a similar manner, mythical images, 'a sign/symbol of roses', chilled almost to the point of being frozen.

The theme of the natural-artificial is also found in the artistic investigations of Pino Pascali, who during these same years 'reconstructed' parts of nature and reinvented animals as characters in his own fantastic bestiary. *Ricostruzione della balena* (*Reconstruction of the Whale*) belongs to this rare series of 'finte sculture' ('fake sculptures') and almost seems to swim like a white fossil on the floor. It's a silent, metaphysical object living in a subtle and ironic give-and-take between the space it fills and the lightness of its own mass.

Pascali, in his brief but dazzling career, hints at the dialogue between the various centers of Italian artistic debate, among which Milan, Turin, and Rome stand out, often seen as distinct loci of experimentation but actually interconnected by numerous exchanges. In 1973, Alighiero Boetti accurately recalled the lively artistic climate in Turin in which Arte Povera (Poor Art) took root:

> By themselves [...] few things occur. On the other hand, to start the ball rolling, one must work as a group. [...] And then, as always happens, each one finds his own way, always clearer and more sharply defined. [...] Thus when Pino Pascali had his 'Cannone' show in 1966 at the Sperone Gallery, it was precisely in Turin that he had the most connections. And Fabro was also in Turin, where he had only few connections. [...] 1967 was an explosive year, for me and for everyone. It was a moment of great excitement, even concerning materials: discovery and enthusiasm for materials that soon brought us to the point of nausea.[8]

The discovery of new materials, always part of a dialogue between nature and artifice, was at the center of Mario Merz and Piero Gilardi's artistic investigations. While Merz visualised the inherent energy of materials using the Fibonacci number sequence, which describes the growth process of many living things, Gilardi, in his natural forms in polyurethane foam, reflects on a possible landscape of the future, completely artificial. The expressive, complex experimentation of the artists grouped together at the end of the 1960s under the name Arte Povera formed a strong conceptual network, as one clearly sees in the work of Alighiero Boetti, Luciano Fabro, Giulio Paolini, and Michelangelo Pistoletto. In *Jasper Johns*, for example, Paolini reflects on the formal and conceptual complexity of the images of the history of art, finding inspiration in *Three Flags*, painted by Johns in 1958 and considered at the time an icon of American New-Dada, a movement in which Johns and Robert Rauschenberg were key figures.

Rauschenberg is one of the artists with whom Peppino Agrati formed a close friendship, and he continued to collect his works from the end of the 1960s through the 1980s. In this show one finds three important works representative of his artistic production during these decades: *Blue Exit*, from 1961, a pictorial masterpiece with an extraordinary compositional and chromatic impact; *Untitled (Scripture III)*, from 1974, linked to the artist's visit to Jerusalem; and *Trasmettitore Argento Glut (Neapolitan)* (*Silver Transmitter Glut [Neapolitan]*) an assemblage of scraps and of apparently insignificant elements given new life in an abstract sculpture of lively sparkle.

From this necessarily brief description, one thing emerges clearly: the dual nature of the Agratis' interest, reflected in their collecting choices, whether of Italian works or American ones. In the collection, pieces coexist in which images play a central role, like the iconicity *par excellence* of Andy Warhol's *Triple Elvis* or the totemic primitiveness of the work of Jean-Michel Basquiat, whom Warhol encouraged and promoted, as well as in major works of the developers of Minimal Art and of American conceptual art. Among these are Richard Serra's 1968 *Prop*, whose melted lead elements are not

welded together and exist in a state of constant tension, or Dan Flavin's *Untitled (To Giuseppe Agrati)* of the same year, dedicated by the artist to Peppino Agrati, one of the first European collectors to understand the importance of Flavin's artistic vision.
Always linked to this conceptual polarity is interest in artistic investigations focused on words and language. In the work of Cy Twombly, one of the original intermediaries between American and Italian art, the suggestive relationship between writing and image is seen in experimenting with new possibilities for the evocative power of painting. On the other hand, with artists like Alighiero Boetti, Vincenzo Agnetti, Joseph Kosuth, and Bruce Nauman, words take a different turn. Even in the choice of techniques one sees a deliberate departure from the creation of works 'by hand' and the demand that art be based only on ideas.
The many paths taken by artistic dialogue, which we have been able to touch upon only briefly here, speak of the Agratis' deep understanding and uncommon capacity for in-depth analysis, seen in a collection that represents a multiplicity of interests in their way of looking at contemporary art. In November 1970, viewed today as a key moment in contemporary art in Milan, the Bulgarian-American artist Christo removed the white cloth in which he had wrapped the Monument to Vittorio Emanuele II in the Piazza del Duomo and placed it over the Monument to Leonardo da Vinci in the Piazza della Scala. The Agrati brothers were present and experienced the event live. Peppino immediately contacted the artist and commissioned him to create works for the garden of his villa in Brianza. He was also one of the patrons of *Valley Curtain*, a monumental orange cloth stretched across the Rifle Gap in Colorado, one of the environmental works that brought Christo fame as a pioneer in Land Art, a current also represented in the collection by important works by Michel Heizer.
The Agratis' passionate understanding of the most significant developments in the art of their time, summarized symbolically in their close relationship with Christo, speaks to us today through the works in this exhibition. The collection is conceived of as revelation and as a way to enrich our souls, sharing the possibility of a world of images that incarnate contemporary life: Luigi and Peppino Agrati's intense love of art.

[1] F. Tedeschi, in *L'arte moderna in Intesa Sanpaolo. La collezione Luigi e Peppino Agrati*, edited by F. Tedeschi, Electa, Milan 2012, p. 11.
[2] *Un folle amore. La collezione Luigi e Peppino Agrati (Madly in Love: The Luigi and Peppino Agrati Collection)*, G. Celant, Skira, Milan 2002, with additional text by Anna Costantini and Silvia Mascheroni.
[3] *L'arte moderna in Intesa Sanpaolo...*, cit., with texts by Francesco Tedeschi and Francesca Pola and entries by Alessia Alberti, Marina degl'Innocenti, Sara Fontana, Isabella Galli, Kevin McManus, Francesco and Francesca Pola, who conducted accurated archive researches preliminary to the classification.
[4] See L. M. Barbero and P. Campiglio, *Lucio Fontana. Teatrini*, exhibition catalogue, Mantova, Casa del Mantegna, July–August 1997, Mantua 1997.
[5] L. Fontana, C. Lonzi, *Autoritratto (Self-portrait)* (1969), Et al., Milan 2010, p. 297.
[6] Cfr. *Azimuth: Continuità e nuovo*, edited by L. M. Barbero, exhibition catalogue, Venice, Peggy Guggenheim Collection, September 24, 2014, to January 15, 2015, Marsilio, Venice 2014.
[7] On this theme: *Imagine: Nuove immagini dell'arte italiana 1960–1969*, edited by L. M. Barbero, exhibition catalogue, Venice, Peggy Guggenheim Collection, April 23 to September 19, 2016, Marsilio, Venice 2016.
[8] M. Bandini, *Torino 1960/1973 (Turin 1960/1973)*, interview with Alighiero Boetti, in 'NAC', no. 3, Rome, March 1963, p. 4.

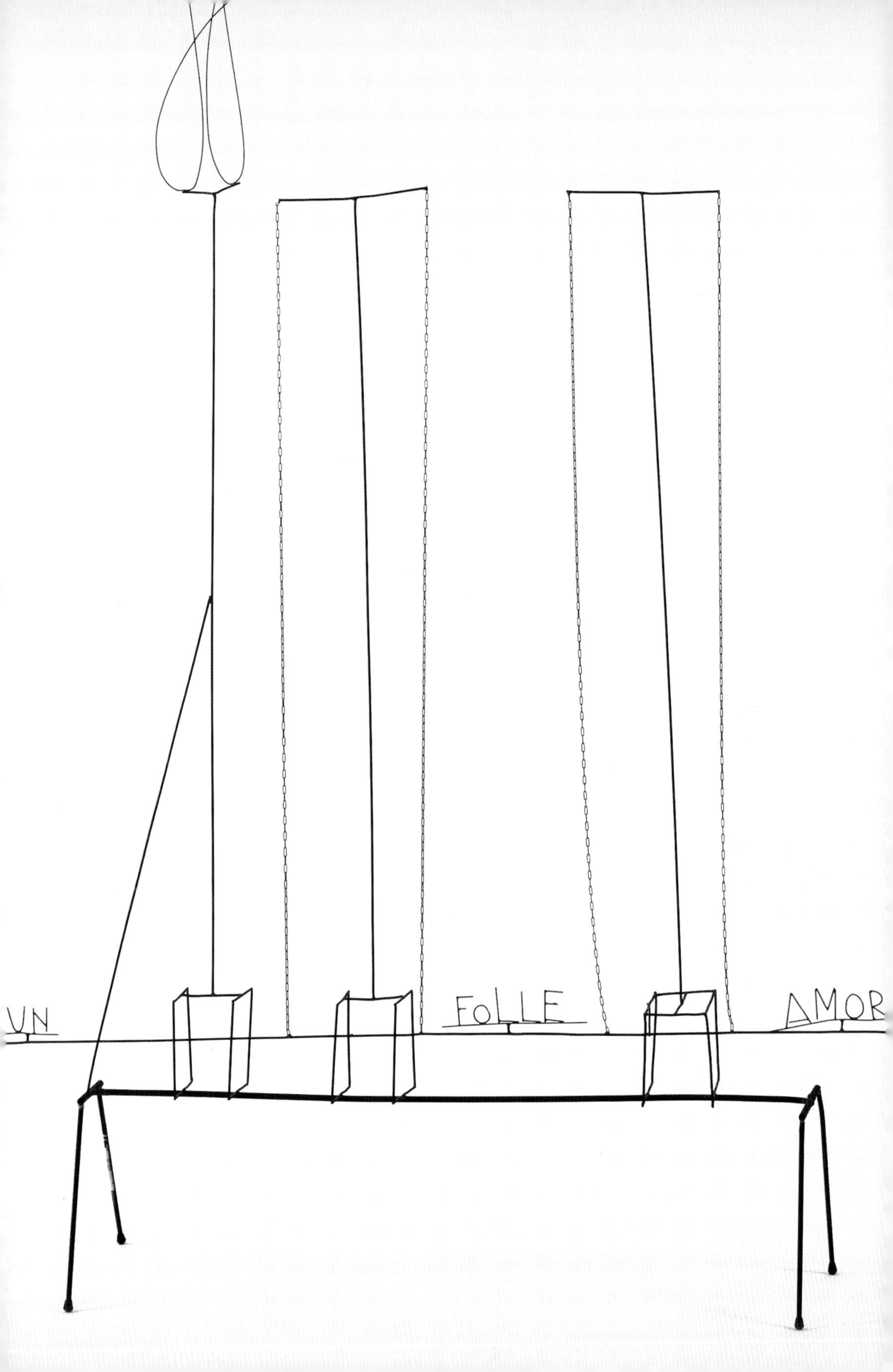
UN
FoLLE
AMOR

FAUSTO MELOTTI:
“A CRAZY LOVE”

CERAMICS ALWAYS HAS A CERTAIN SPRINGLIKE POVERTY.
IT'S *ARTE POVERA* AND PAUPERS' ART DRESSED IN ALL ITS FINERY.
A GENTLE POPULAR RETALIATION.

FAUSTO MELOTTI

In *Fausto Melotti*, edited by Germano Celant, exhibition catalogue (Venice, Palazzo Fortuny, March-June 1990), Electa, Milan 1990

FAUSTO MELOTTI
Rovereto 1901 – Milan 1986

Kore, ca. 1955
glazed ceramic
h 101 cm

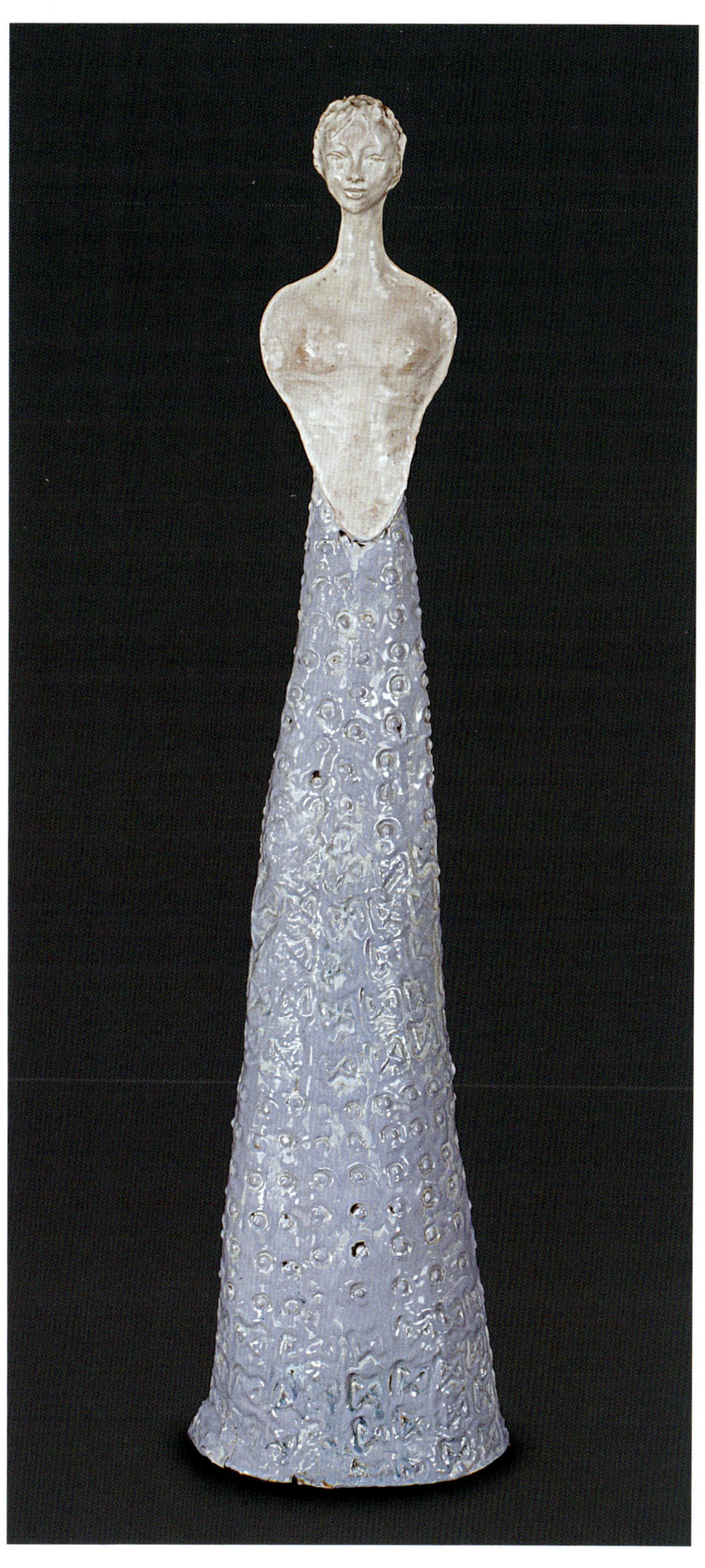

FAUSTO MELOTTI
Rovereto 1901 – Milan 1986

Kore, ca. 1955
glazed ceramic
h 101 cm

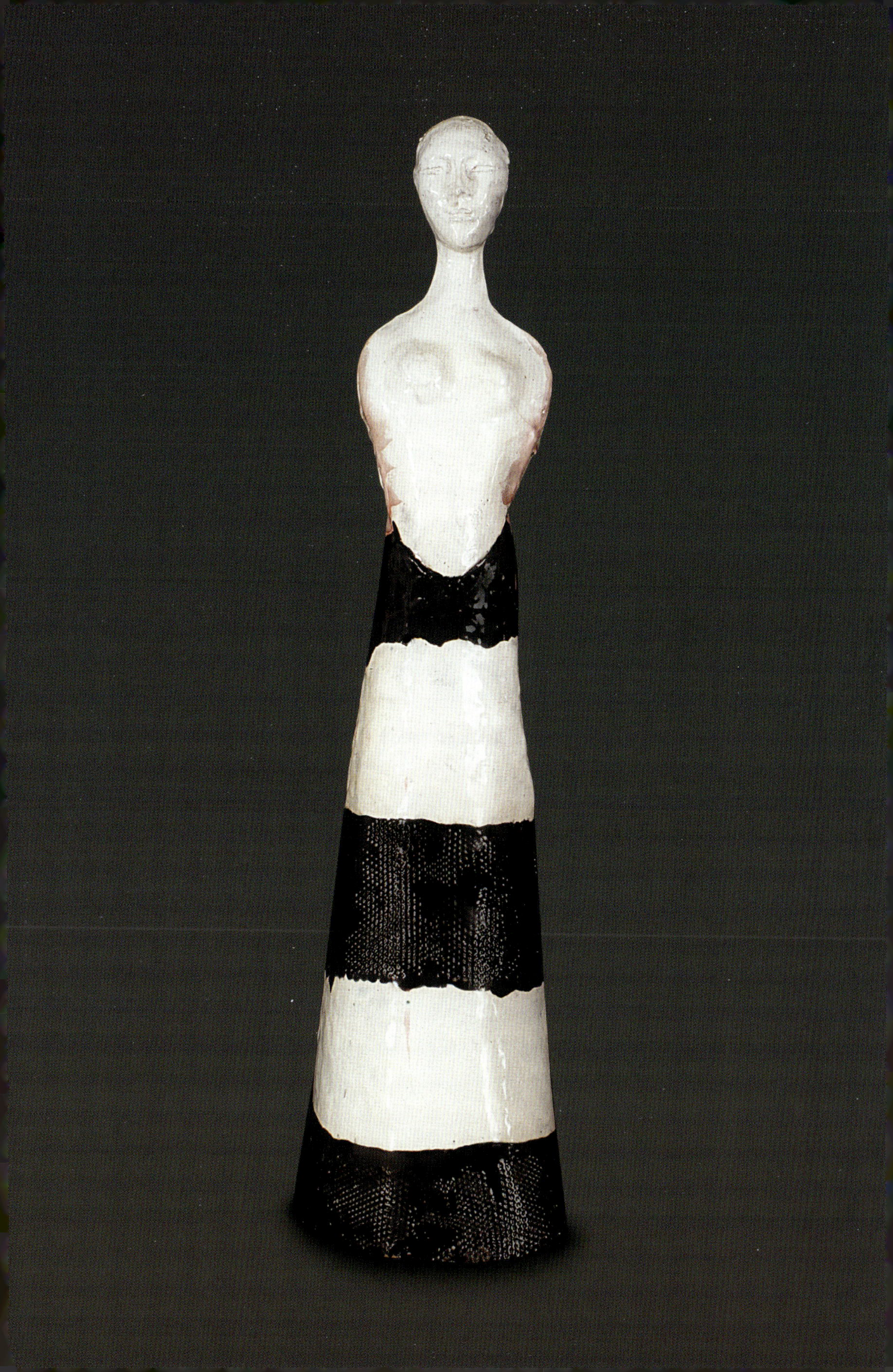

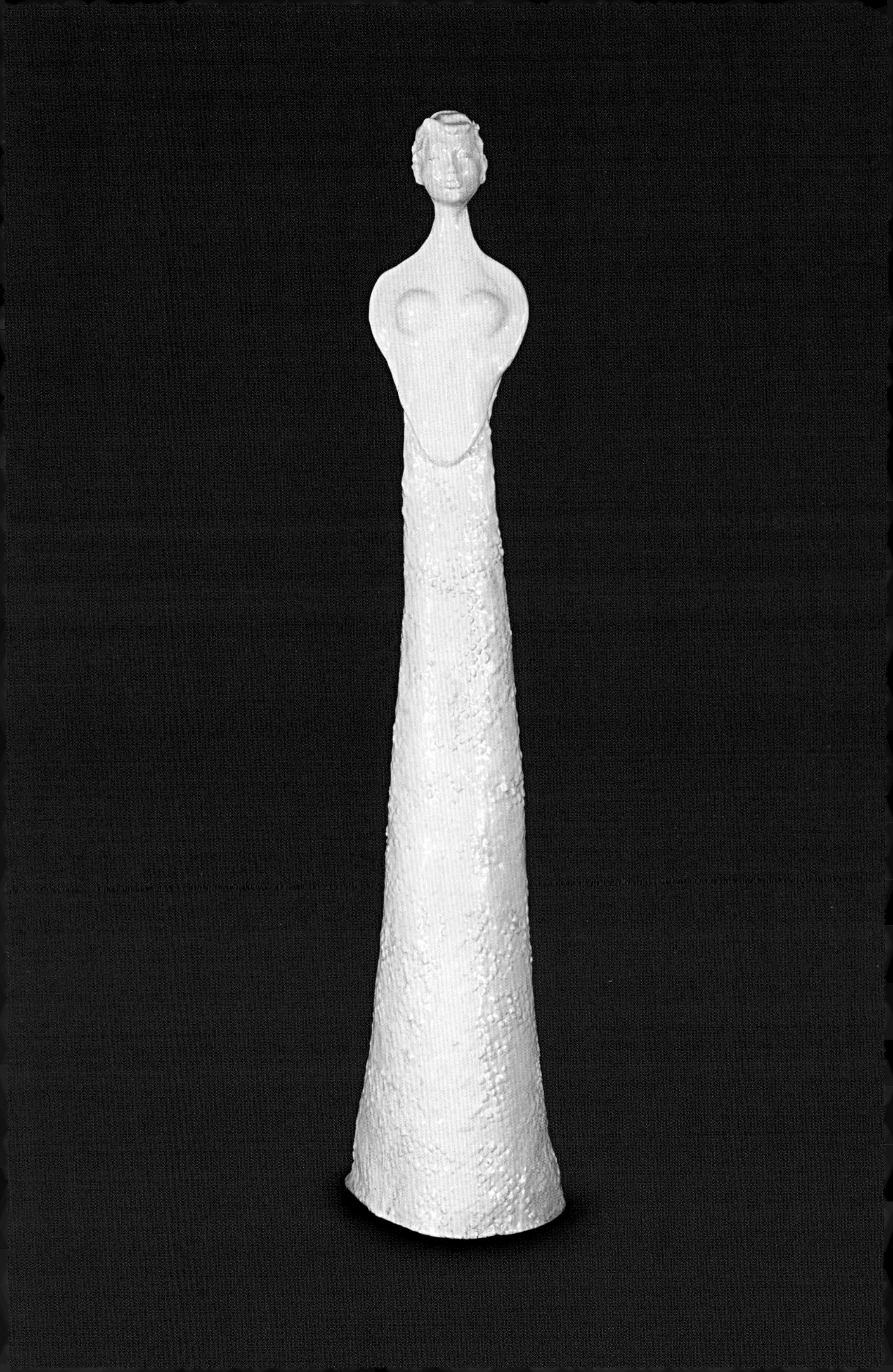

FAUSTO MELOTTI
Rovereto 1901 – Milan 1986

Kore, 1955-1956
glazed ceramic
h 100 cm

Kore, 1955-1956
glazed ceramic
h 108 cm

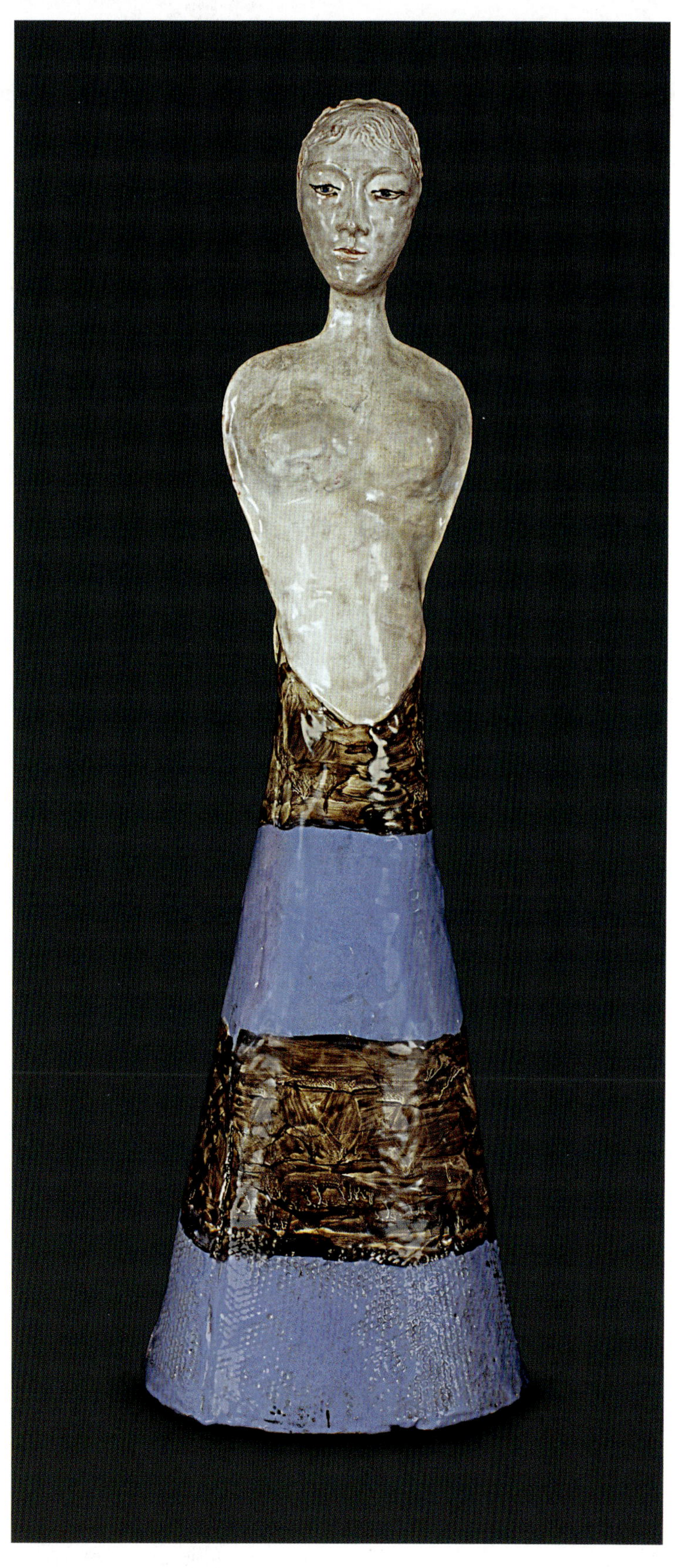

THAT IN ORDER TO VISIT MELOTTI'S STUDIO IT IS NECESSARY TO PASS THROUGH A TRAP DOOR AND CLIMB AND DESCEND A SUBMARINE-LIKE STAIRCASE, IS A FACT NOT TO BE OVERLOOKED [. . .] BECAUSE EVERY COGNITIVE JOURNEY CANNOT BUT BEGIN WITH A STEEP VERTICAL DISLOCATION [. . .]. NO LONGER SUBMERGED BY THEIR WIDTH AND MECHANISMS, THE RAREFIED SCAFFOLDINGS OF HAPPINESS RISE ON A HORIZON THAT HAS BEEN REMOVED FROM THE GAY EYES OF THE TRAVELLER. BUT THE SMILE OF THE WISE MAN WHO GUIDES HIM, AS LIGHT AS AN ELDERLY ANGEL AND PERCEPTIVE AS AN AUGURAL CHILD, WARNS HIM THAT THIS VEGETATION OF DISEMBODIED SIGNS IS ROOTED IN OUR PRECARIOUS LIFE ON THIS PLANET: THIS CONCERT OF PERCUSSION BEATS AND FLUTE TRILLS IS THE ONLY WAY TO EXPRESS SADNESS IN THE FACE OF THE IMPOSSIBLE POSSIBLES [. . .]. WE DO NOT KNOW WHETHER AT THE END OF THE JOURNEY THE TRAVELLER WILL GRASP THE ULTIMATE ESSENCES, THE IDEOGRAMS OF AN ABSOLUTE ALPHABET, BUT UNDOUBTEDLY HE WILL SEE AN INVENTORY OF THREE-DIMENSIONAL AND DYNAMIC EMBLEMS, EACH OF THEM HOISTED ON A STAND, READY TO SING LIKE LITTLE UMBRELLAS, TO UNCOIL LIKE SPRINGS, TO FLUTTER LIKE TAILS OF A KITE. AND AMONG OTHER FESTIVE SIGNS, HIS EYE WILL ALSO CAPTURE THE SHAPE OF A PITCHFORK, SLENDER AND PRIMORDIAL LIKE A CHILDLIKE INSCRIPTION.

ITALO CALVINO

I segni alti, in *Fausto Melotti. Lo spazio inquieto*, edited by Paolo Fossati, Einaudi, Turin 1971

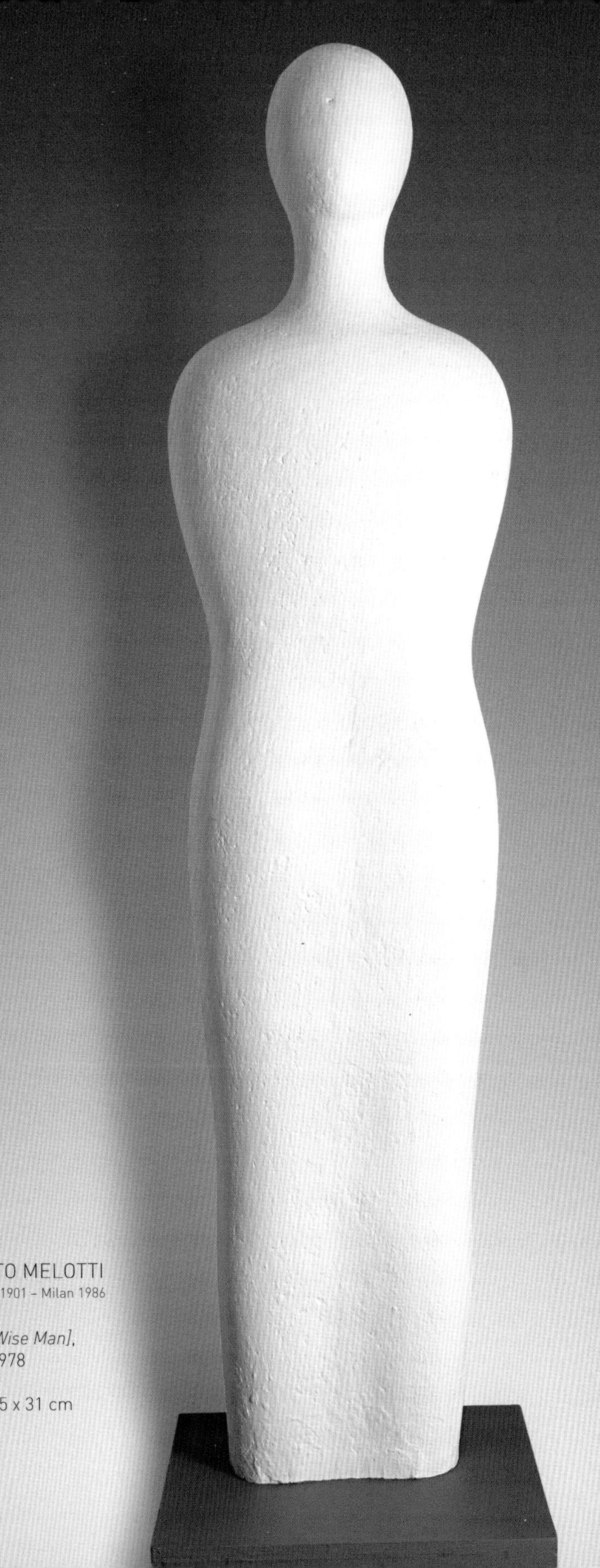

FAUSTO MELOTTI
Rovereto 1901 – Milan 1986

Savio [Wise Man],
1960-1978
plaster
225 x 55 x 31 cm

FAUSTO MELOTTI
Rovereto 1901 – Milan 1986

Senza titolo
(I giocolieri) [Untitled
(The Jugglers)],
1959-1960
brass
37,1 x 12 x 9 cm

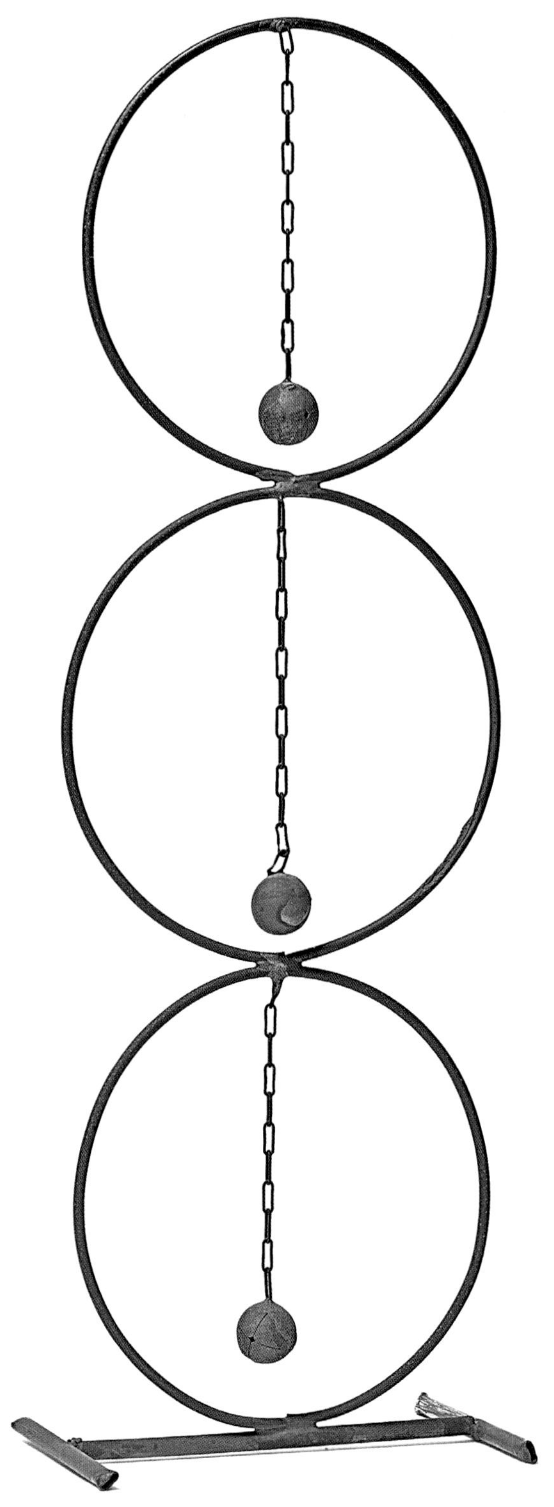

FAUSTO MELOTTI
Rovereto 1901 – Milan 1986

Il carro [The Cart],
1966
brass
243 x 160 x 45 cm

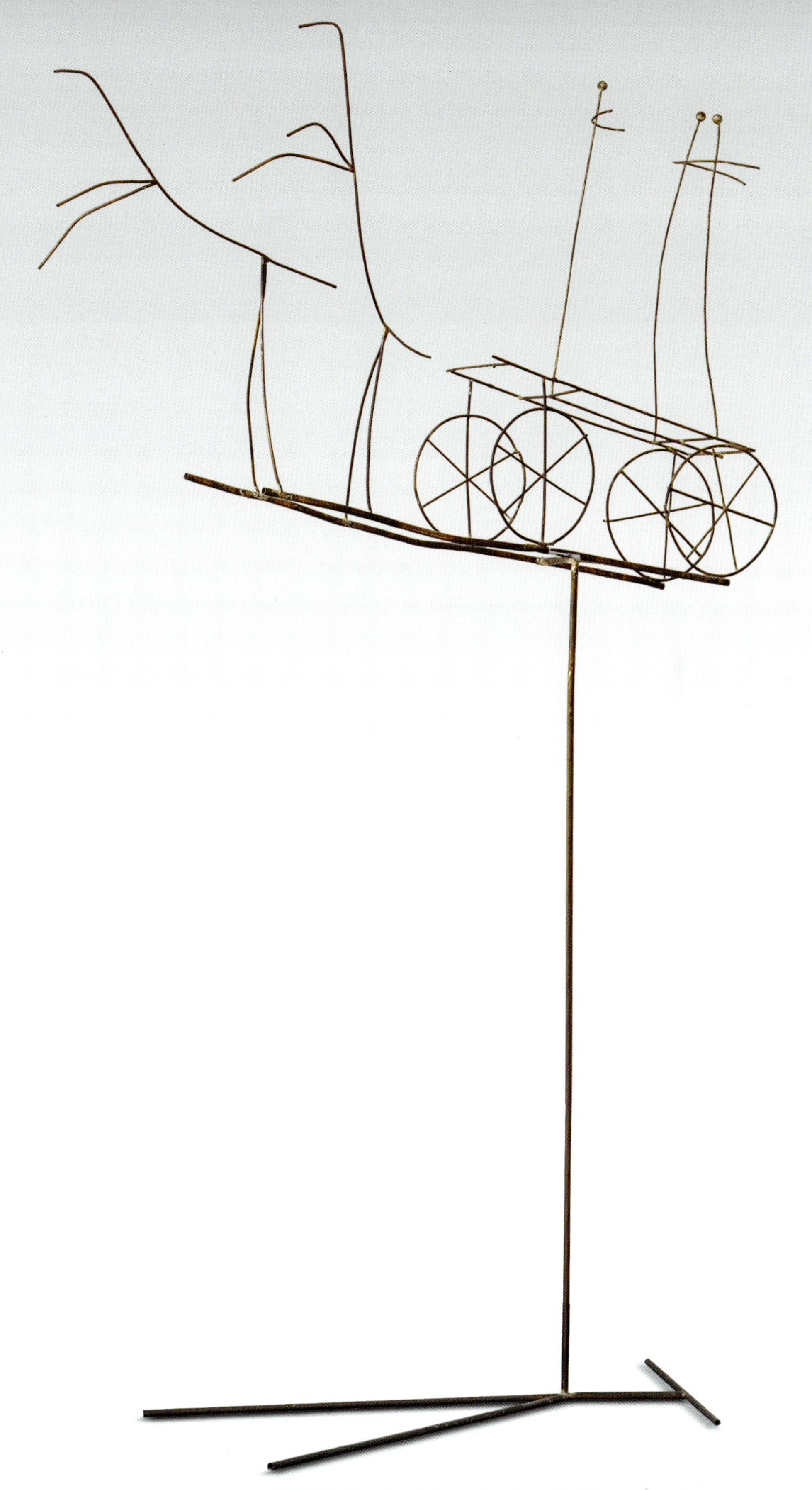

MELOTTI RETURNED TO SCULPTURE IN THE LATE FIFTIES, AFTER A LONG PERIOD SPENT DEVOTING HIMSELF ALMOST EXCLUSIVELY TO CERAMICS. THE ARTIST BEGAN EXPERIMENTING WITH DUCTILE METALS LIKE BRASS, WITH WHICH HE DREW DELICATE, AERIAL FIGURES IN SPACE, ACCORDING TO AN IDEA OF SHAPE MODULATION SIMILAR TO THAT OF A MUSICAL COMPOSITION. MELOTTI CREATED AN OPEN SCULPTURE CHARACTERISED BY EXTREME SYNTHESES AND STYLISATIONS – A "SENSE OF LEVITY", ALMOST AN "ANTI-SCULPTURE". EMPTIED OF ALL WEIGHT, TRACES IN SPACE SEEMINGLY BECOME UNSTABLE AND MOBILE, TAKING ON A DIMENSION AT ONCE POETIC, FAIRYTALE-LIKE AND NARRATIVE. LIKE THE OTHER WORKS BY MELOTTI WE FIND IN THE LUIGI E PEPPINO AGRATI COLLECTION, THESE CREATIONS ATTEST TO THE INTENSE, PROFOUND RAPPORT ESTABLISHED BETWEEN COLLECTOR AND ARTIST.

FAUSTO MELOTTI
Rovereto 1901 – Milan 1986

Carro II [The Cart II],
1969
brass
100 x 30 x 12 cm

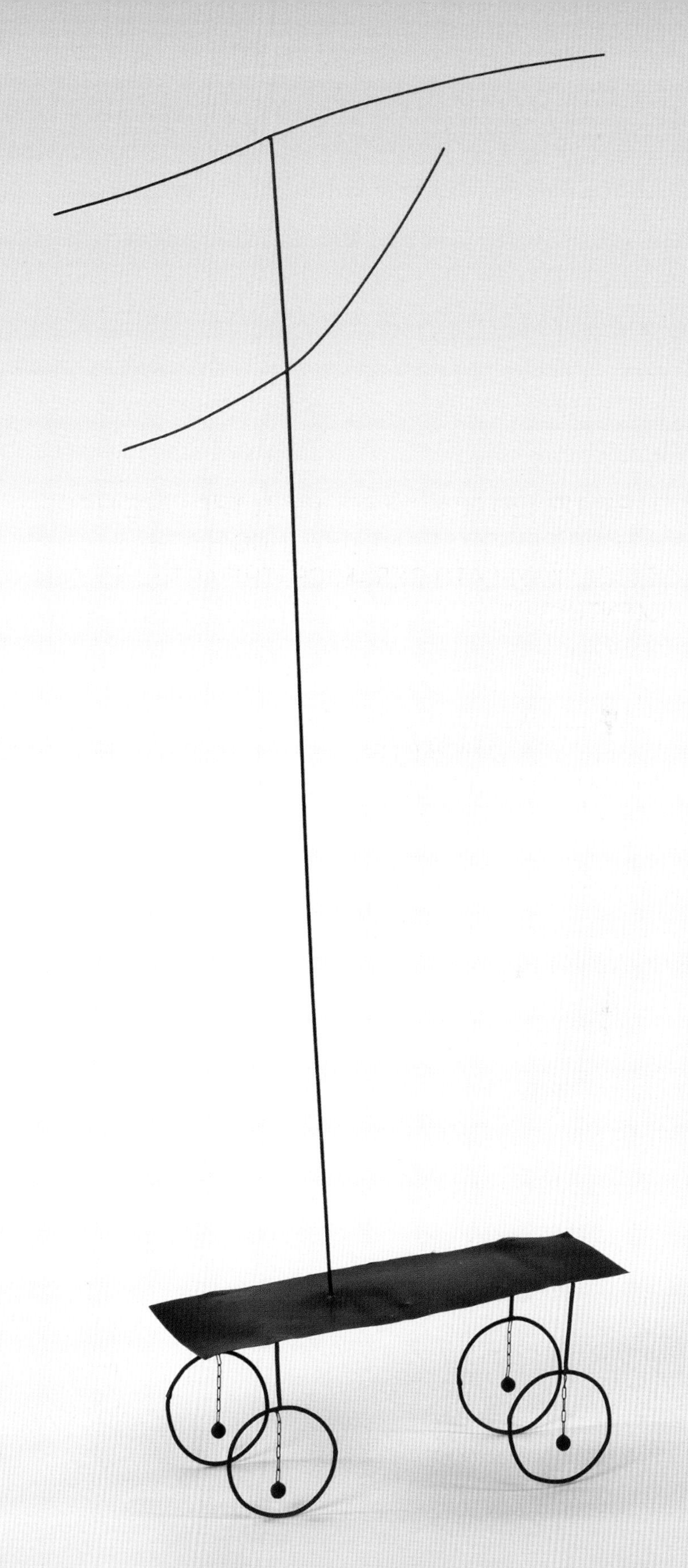

FAUSTO MELOTTI
Rovereto 1901 – Milan 1986

Un folle amore
[A Crazy Love], 1971
brass
130 x 110 x 40 cm

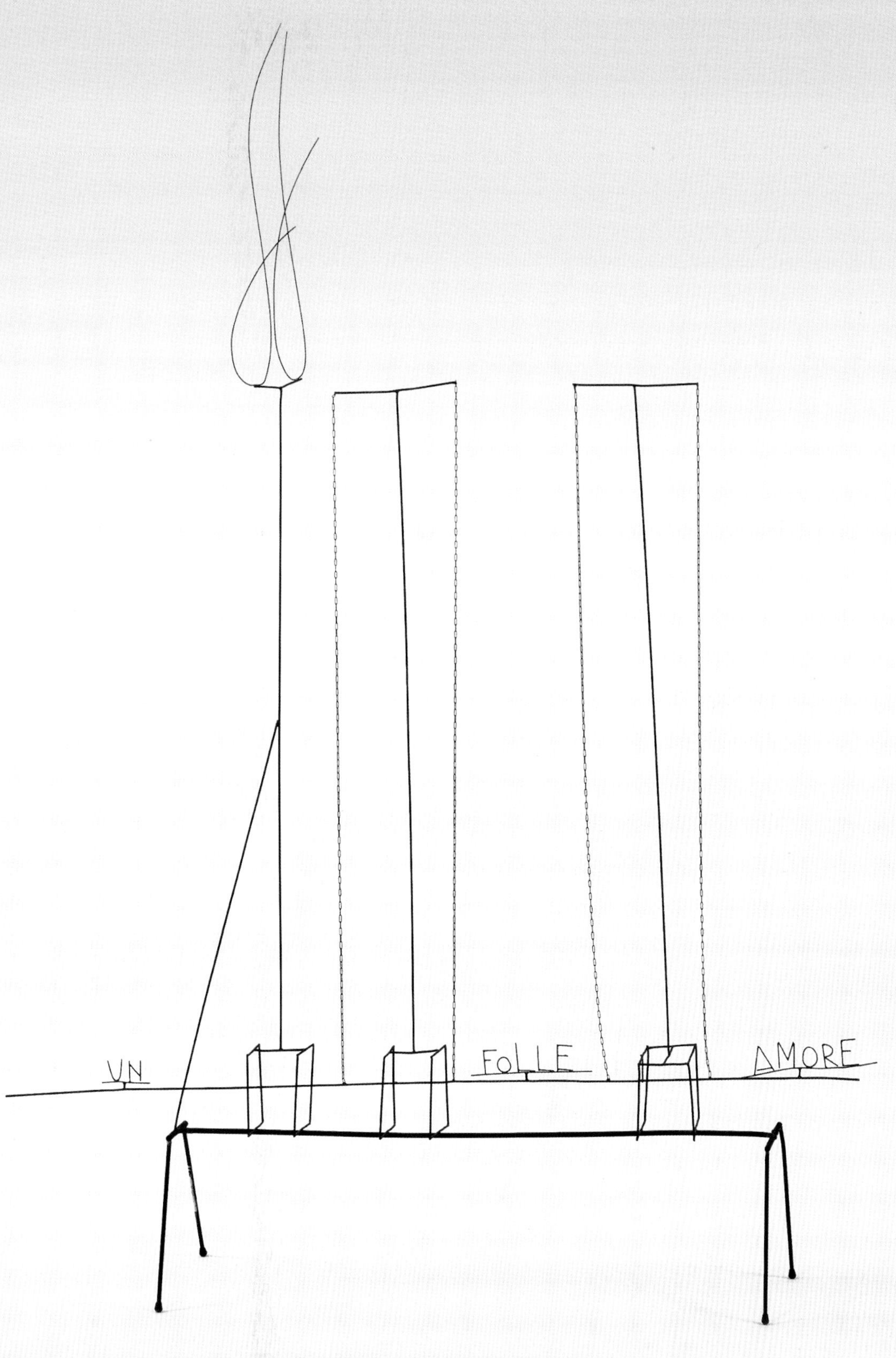
UN
FOLLE
AMORE

FAUSTO MELOTTI
Rovereto 1901 – Milan 1986

L'indeciso
[The Hesitant], 1974
stainless steel
200 x 72 x 72 cm

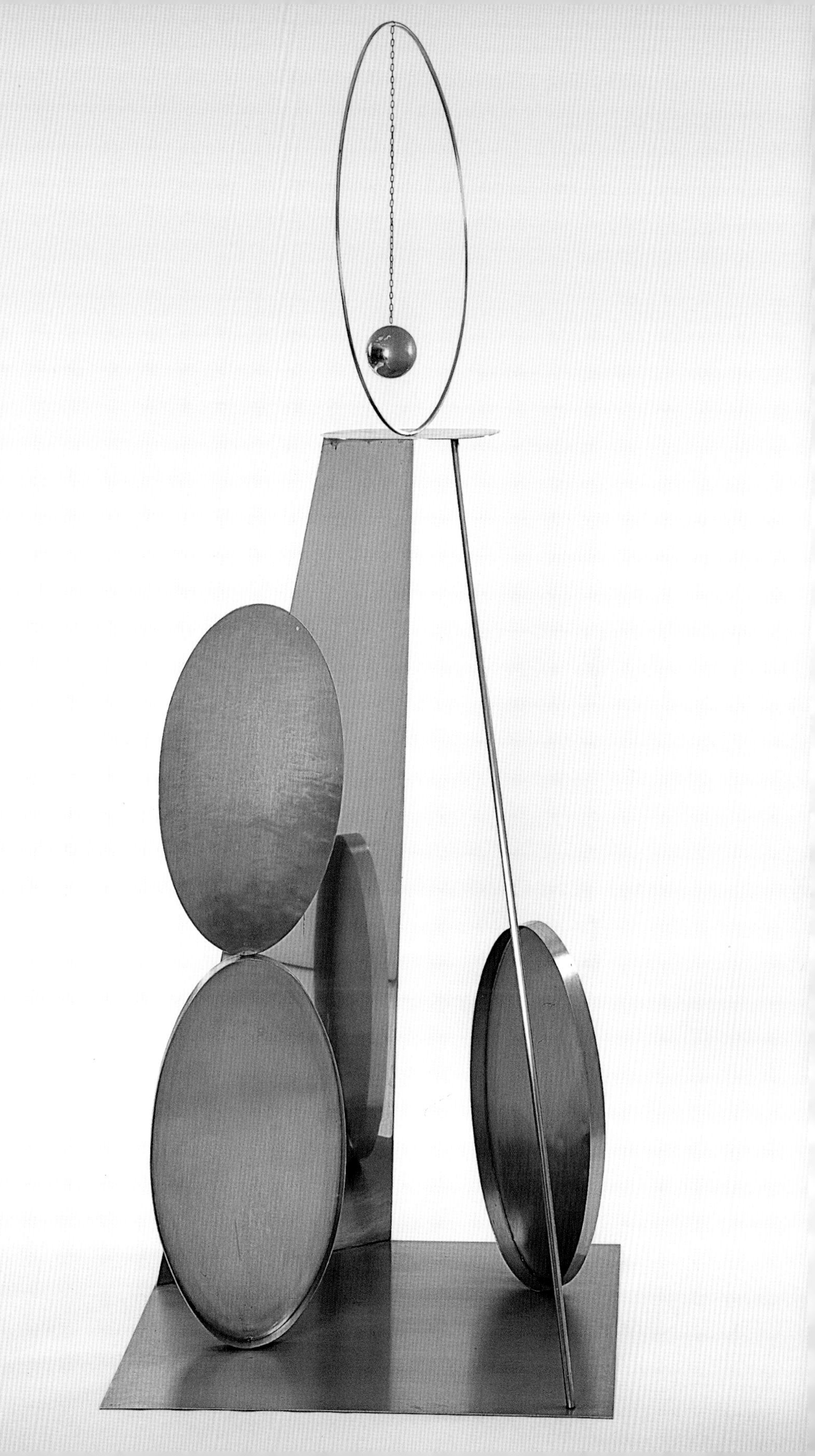

FAUSTO MELOTTI
Rovereto 1901 – Milan 1986

Il riposo del re [The Rest of the King], 1975
brass
47 x 51 x 11 cm

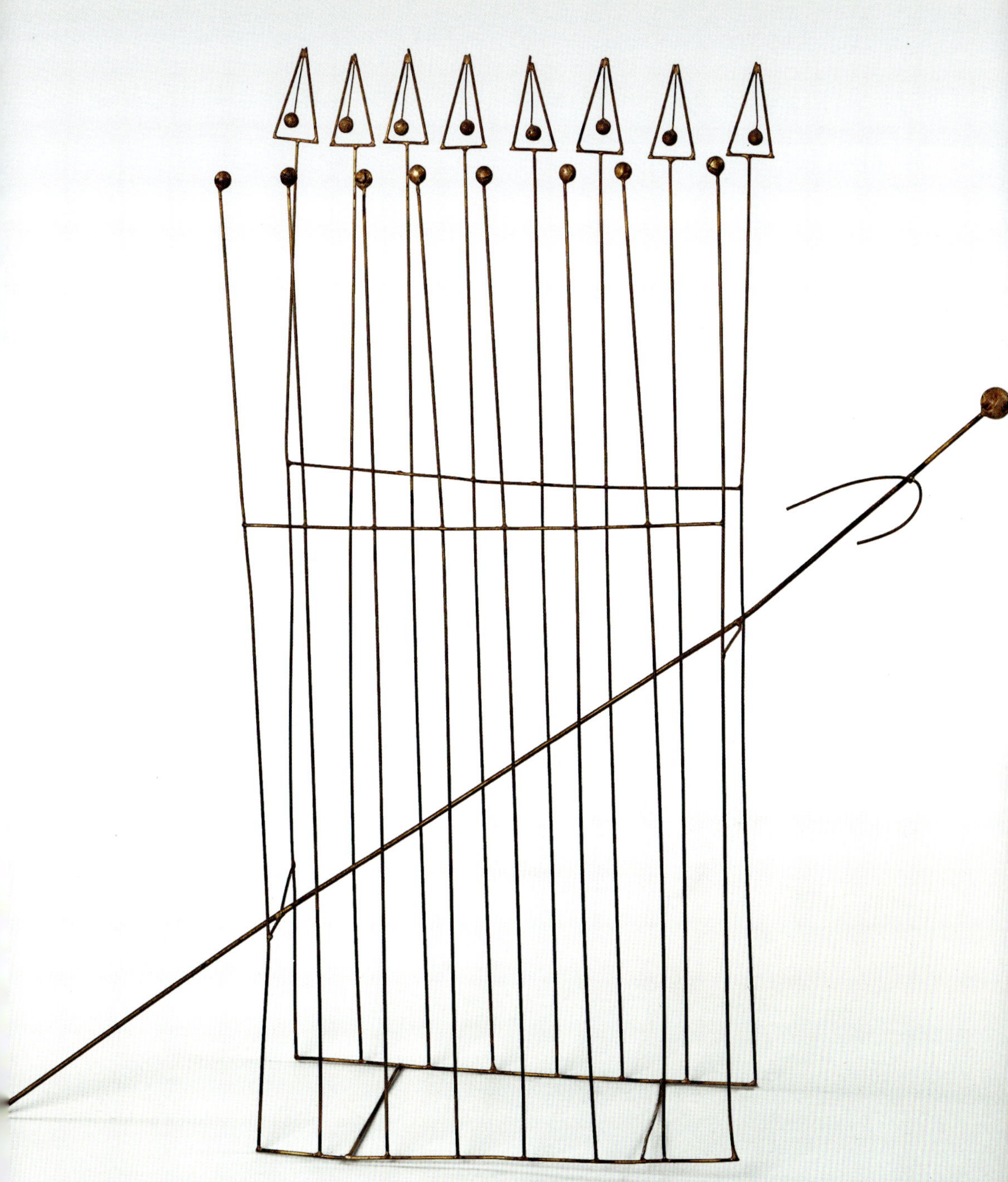

FAUSTO MELOTTI
Rovereto 1901 – Milan 1986

Gli specchi [The Mirrors], 1975
brass
40 x 91 x 7,5 cm

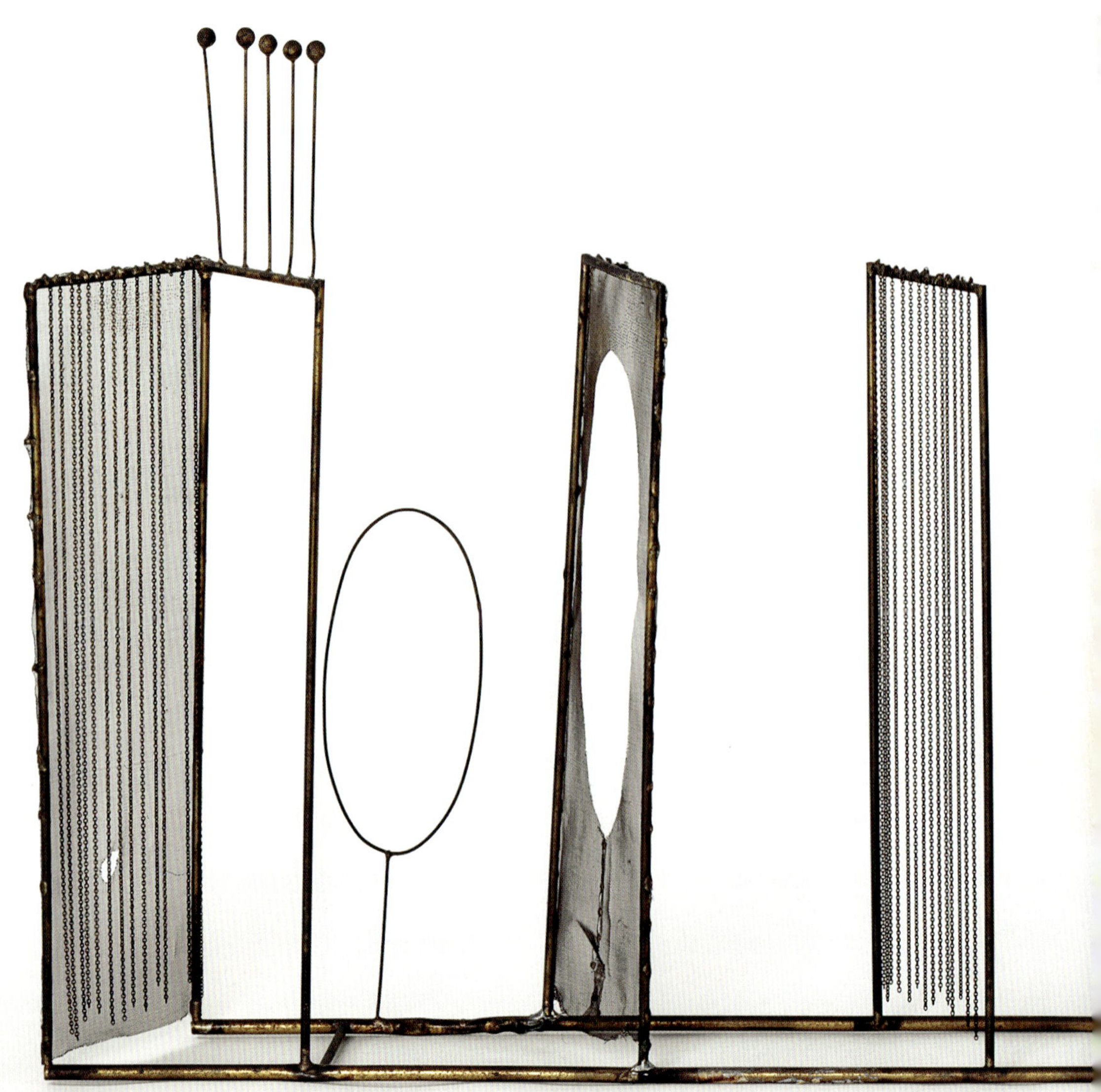

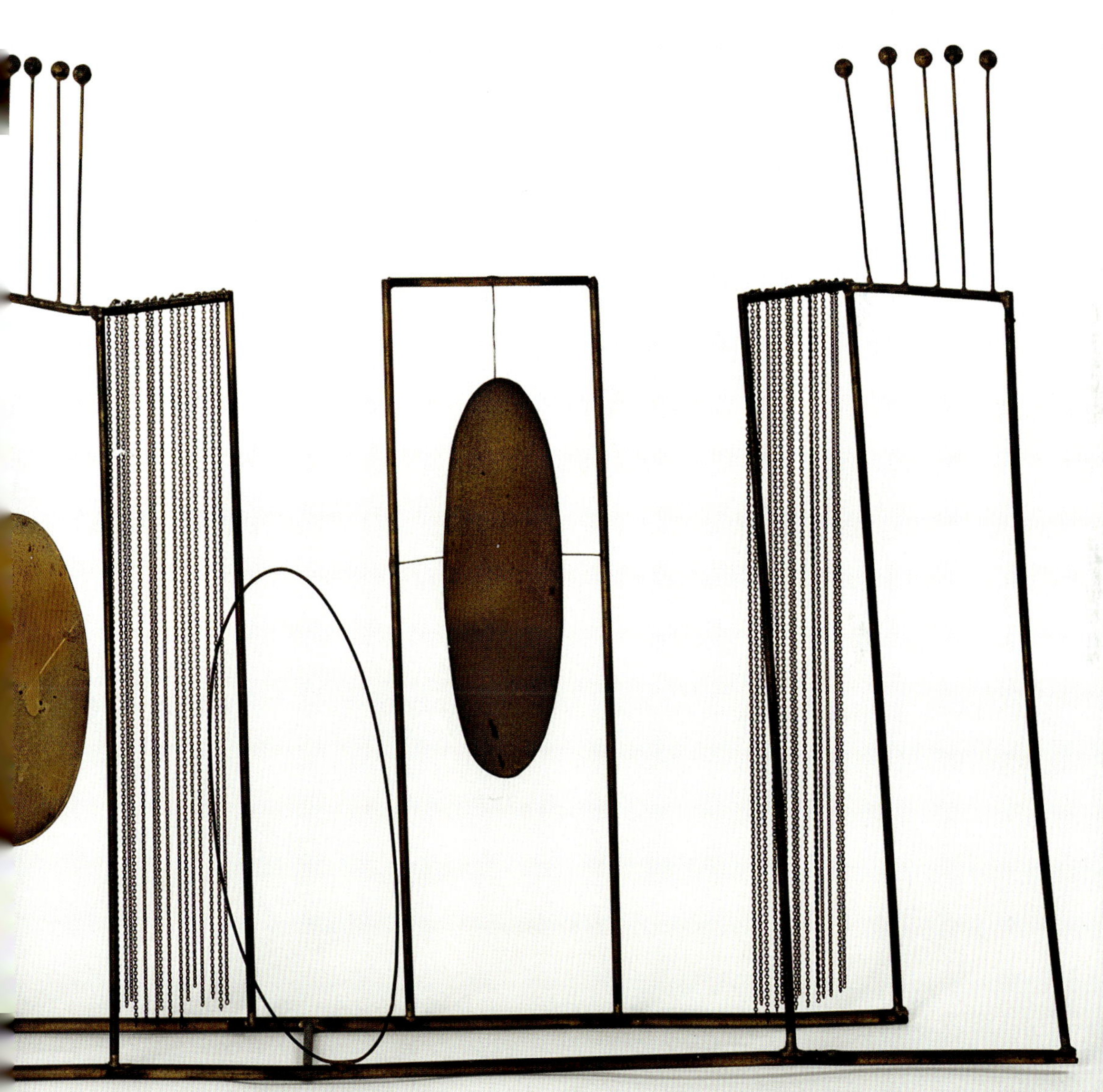

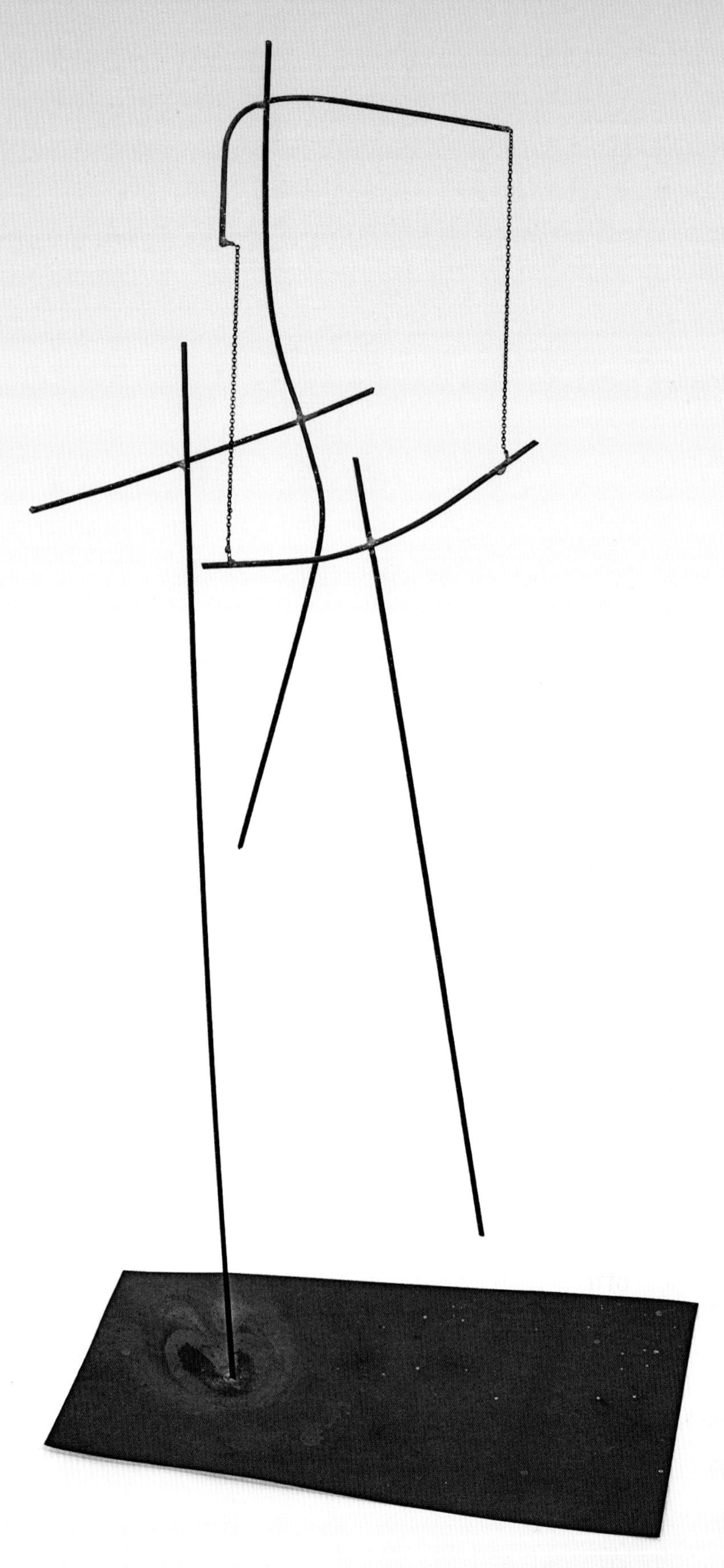

ART DOES NOT REPRESENT,
IT TRANSFORMS REALITY INTO SYMBOLS.
SHOCK MAY BE A POINT OF DEPARTURE,
BUT ART IS A JOURNEY.

FAUSTO MELOTTI

Linee, Adelphi, Milan 1981

FAUSTO MELOTTI
Rovereto 1901 – Milan 1986

Deposizione [The Deposition], 1975
brass
65 x 27 x 17 cm

FAUSTO MELOTTI
Rovereto 1901 – Milan 1986

Spensierata [Carefree],
1976
brass
69 x 55 x 65 cm

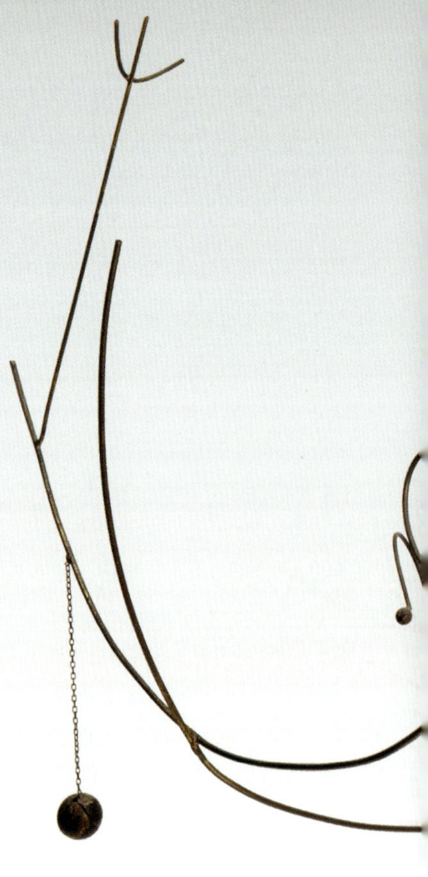

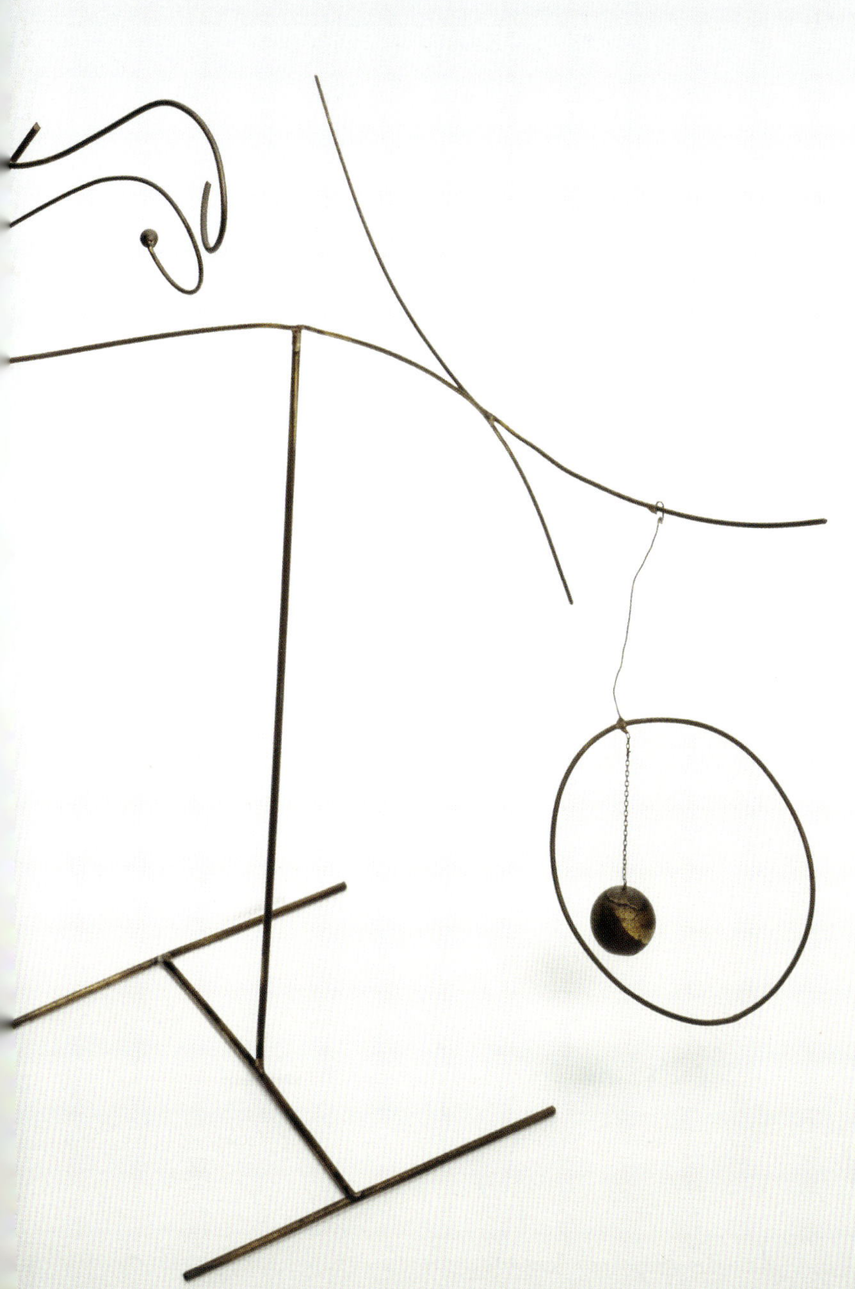

FAUSTO MELOTTI
Rovereto 1901 – Milan 1986

Senza titolo [Untitled],
1977
plaster, brass,
tempera, charcoal
70 x 50 x 7 cm

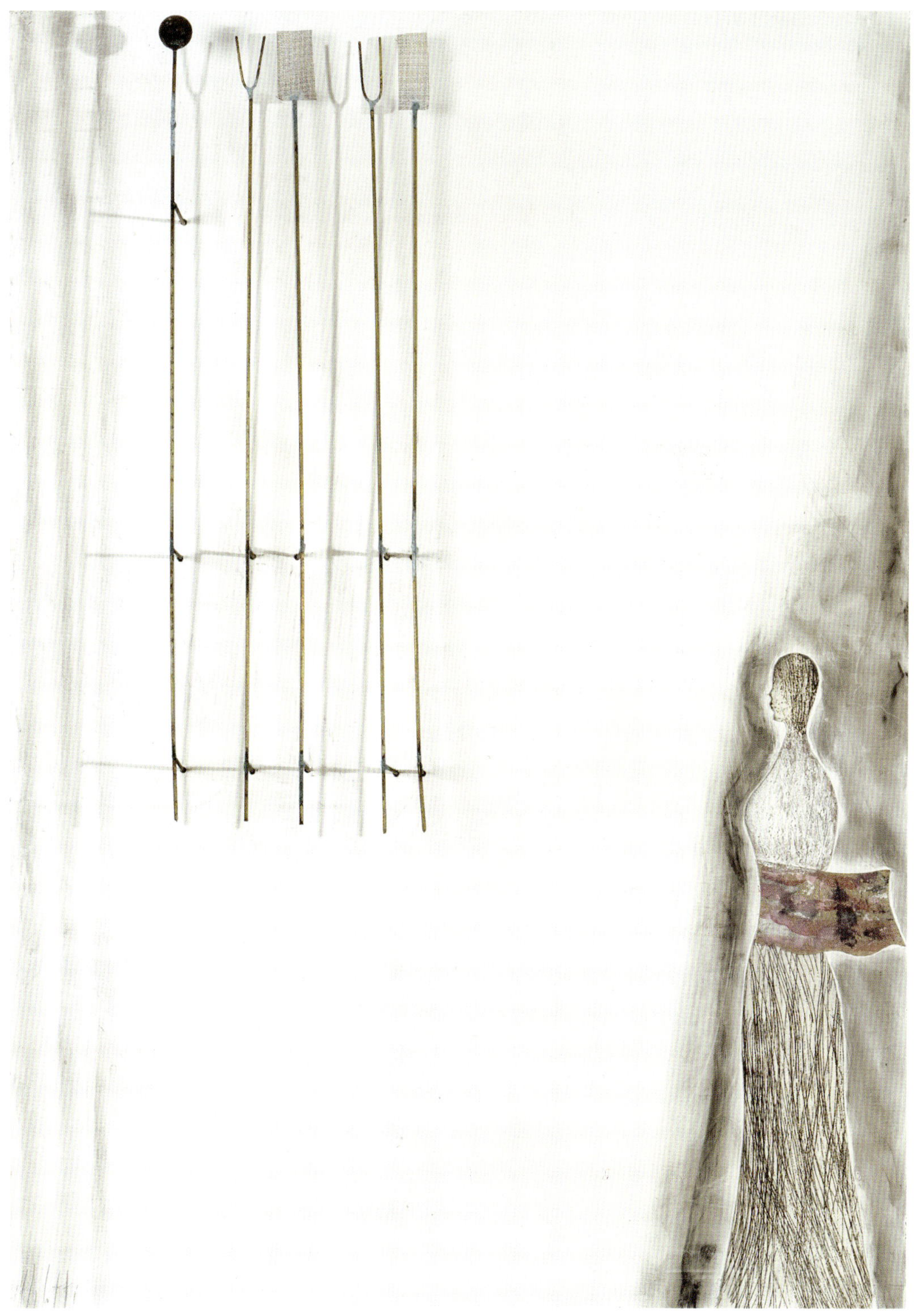

FAUSTO MELOTTI
Rovereto 1901 – Milan 1986

Dentro [Inside], 1977
brass
62 x 62 x 33,5 cm

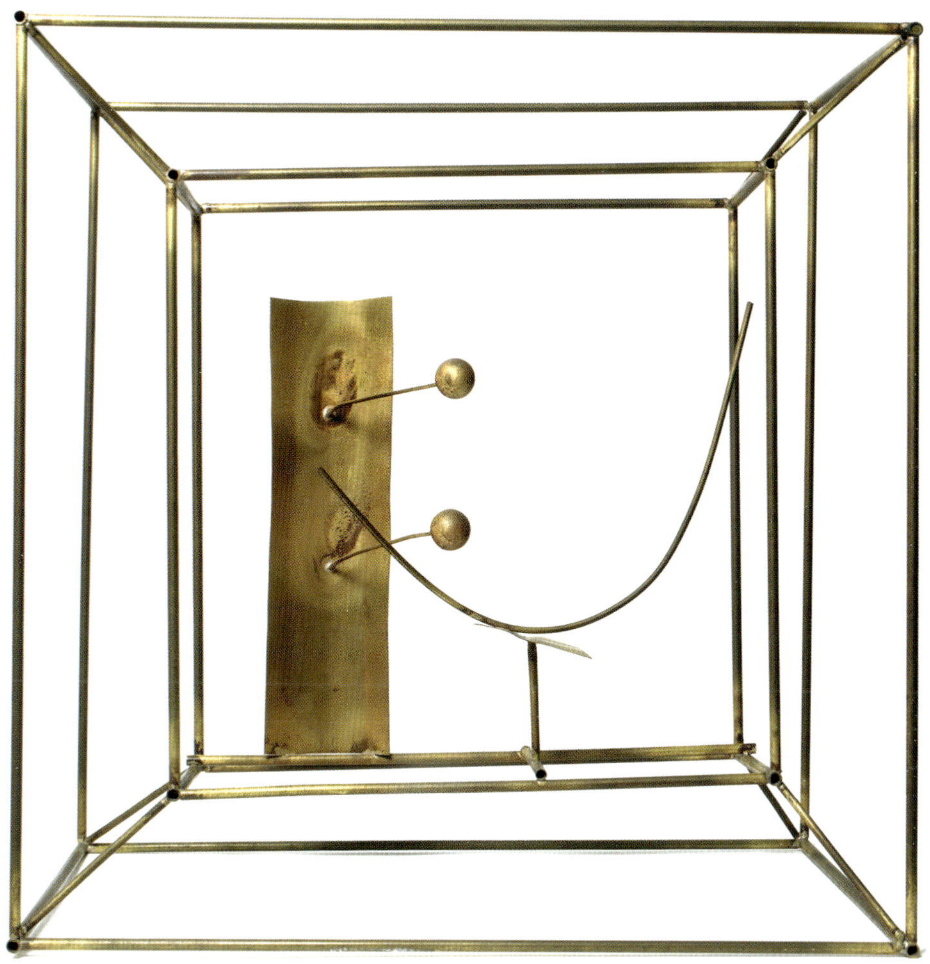

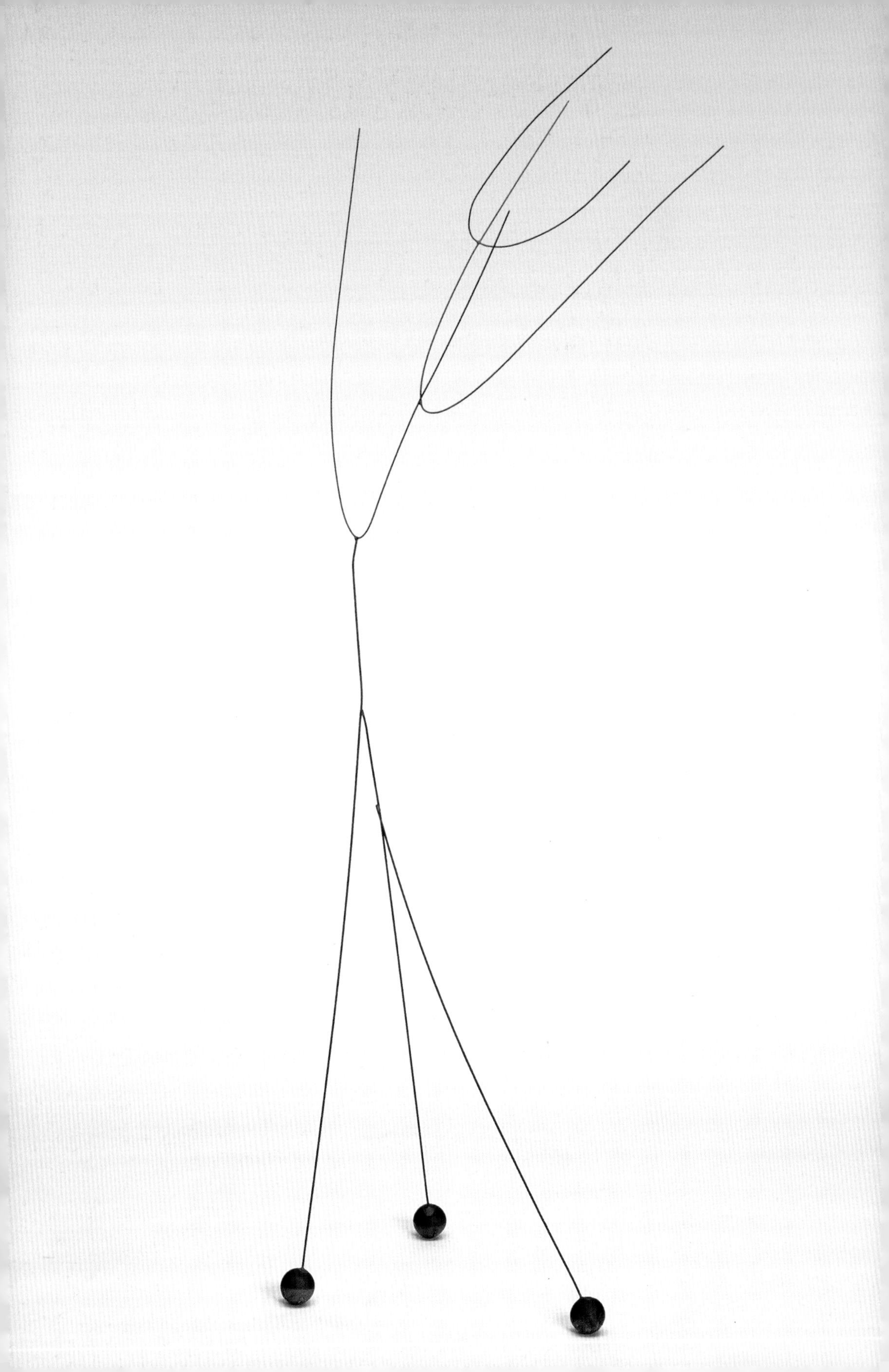

FAUSTO MELOTTI
Rovereto 1901 – Milan 1986

U, 1977
brass
108 x 33 x 21 cm

La zingara [The Gypsy Woman], 1980
brass, painted fabric
74 x 22 cm

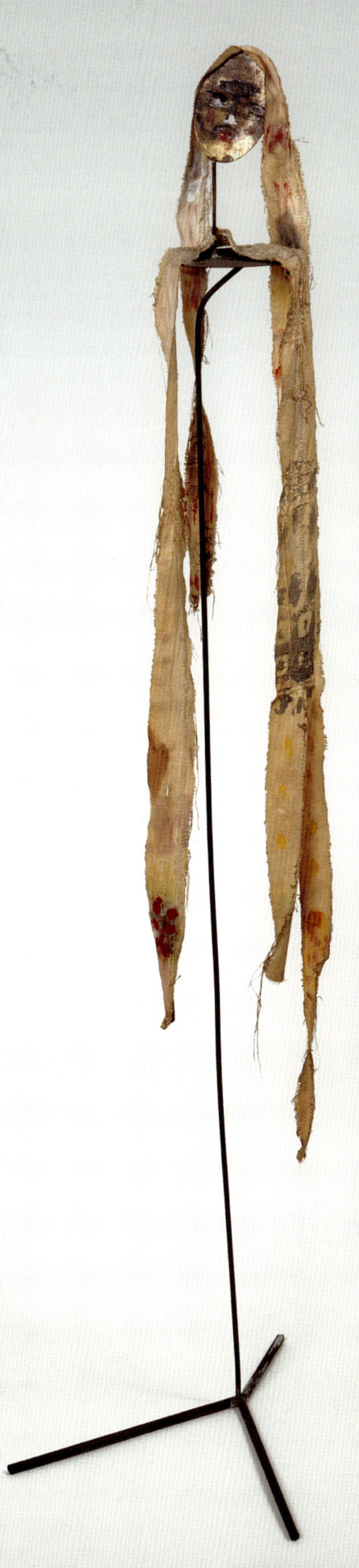

ELIMINATE THE PLEASURE, THE APPETITE FOR MATERIAL.
IN SCULPTURE, WHAT COUNTS IS THE HARMONIC OCCUPATION OF SPACE, IN PAINTING THE PROFOUND PLAY OF DRAWING AND COLOUR.
THE FLEETING SURPRISES OF MATERIAL ARE NOT THE DREAM.
STAINS ON THE WALL CAN ONLY BE A BEGINNING OF THE DREAM.

FAUSTO MELOTTI

Linee, Adelphi, Milan 1981

FAUSTO MELOTTI
Rovereto 1901 – Milan 1986

Senza titolo [Untitled],
ca. 1981
brass, mirror
106 x 10 x 15 cm

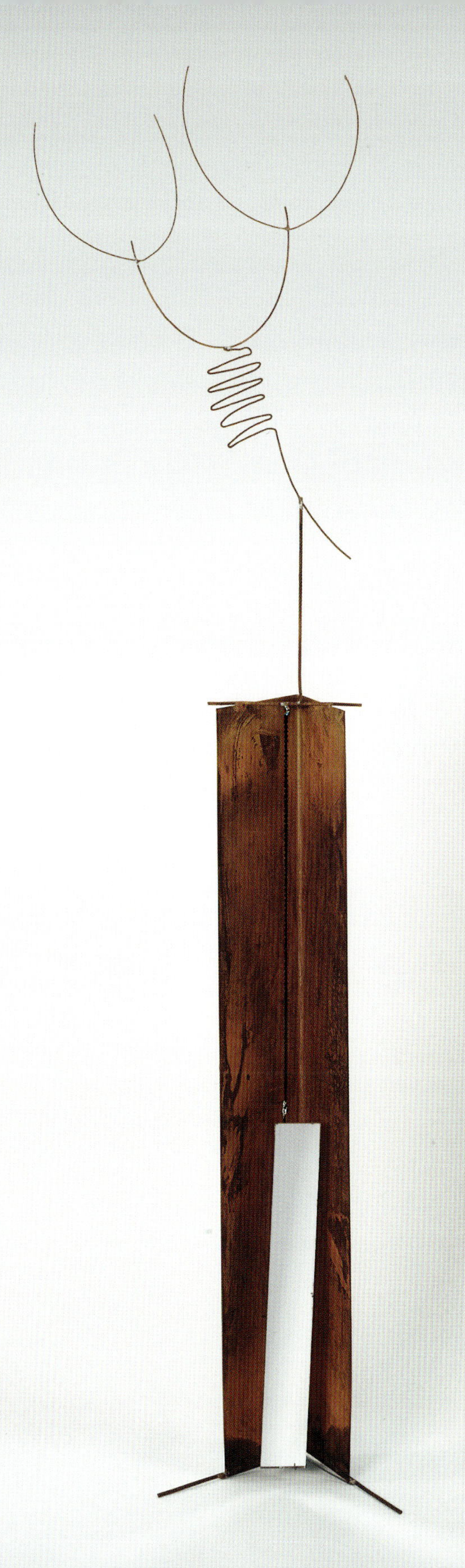

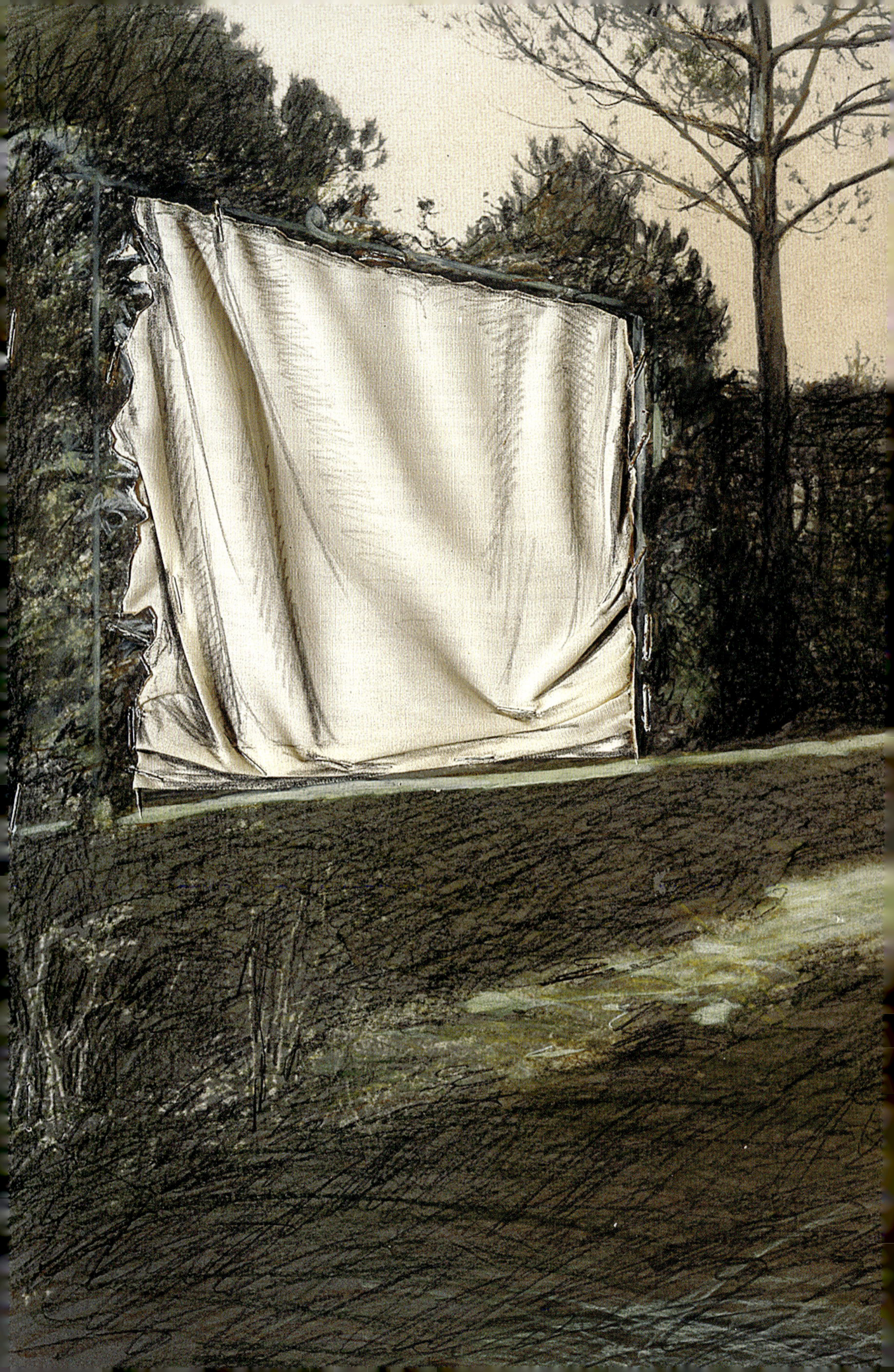

CHRISTO:
MILAN AND THE AGRATI GARDEN

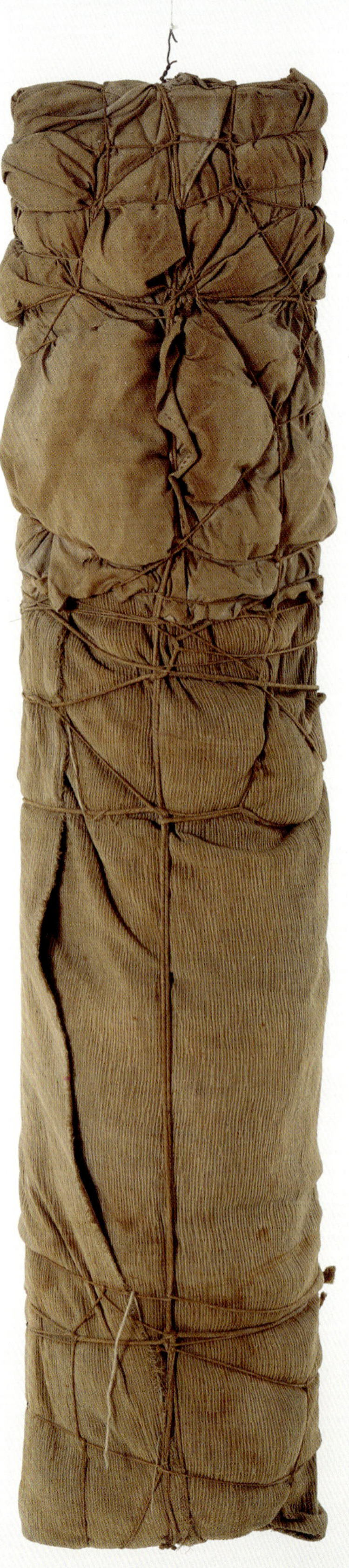

CHRISTO
(CHRISTO
JAVACHEFF)
Gabrovo 1935

Package, ca. 1961
fabric, rope, jute
128 x 30 x 23 cm

IN NOVEMBER 1970, CHRISTO WAS IN MILAN WHERE HE WAS WORKING AT A SOLO EXHIBITION WHILE ALSO PREPARING A PROJECT FOR THE FESTIVAL OF NOUVEAU RÉALISME ORGANISED BY ART CRITIC PIERRE RESTANY TO CELEBRATE THE TENTH ANNIVERSARY OF THE FOUNDATION OF THE GROUP OF THE SAME NAME. THE FESTIVAL, WHICH HAS GONE DOWN IN HISTORY AS ONE OF THE MOMENTOUS EPISODES OF CONTEMPORARY ART IN MILAN, SAW THE PARTICIPATION OF ARTISTS SUCH AS ARMAN, CÉSAR, ROTELLA, SPOERRI, AND TINGUELY, WITH PROJECTS THAT ENLIVENED MANY PUBLIC SPACES OF THE CITY. OVER SPRING AND SUMMER, CHRISTO HAD PRESENTED HIS IDEA OF WRAPPING THE ARCO DELLA PACE, BUT THE CITY OF MILAN REJECTED THE IDEA OF LETTING HIM USE THAT IMPORTANT GATE. RATHER SURPRISINGLY, HOWEVER, CHRISTO WAS GIVEN THE AUTHORISATION TO WRAP THE VITTORIO EMANUELE STATUE IN PIAZZA DEL DUOMO, A MONUMENT THAT WAS EVEN MORE CENTRAL AND EMBLEMATIC. THE FESTIVAL INAUGURATED WITH CHRISTO'S WRAPPED MONUMENT GENERATING VIVID REACTIONS AS THE ARTIST HIMSELF REMEMBERED, "THERE WAS A STRIKE AT PIRELLI, THE TIRE MANUFACTURER. MEMBERS OF THEIR ALL-COMMUNIST UNION MARCHED AROUND WITH FLAGS AND SIGNS, USING THE WRAPPED MONUMENT AS A PLATFORM TO MAKE SPEECHES. IT WAS A PERFECT PLACE. THE EVENT TOOK ON A POLITICAL EDGE."[1]
DUE TO THE HEATED PROTESTS AND PICKETS ORGANISED BY VETERANS, THE SCULPTURE WAS UNVEILED AND THE WHITE SHEET REUSED TO COVER THE MONUMENT TO LEONARDO DA VINCI IN PIAZZA DELLA SCALA. THIS MEANINGFUL PRESENCE OF CHRISTO IN MILAN GAVE RISE TO THE DEEP BOND WITH PEPPINO AGRATI, WHICH WOULD LAST FOR YEARS.

[1] In Burt Chernow, *XTO + J-C. Christo e Jeanne-Claude. Una biografia*, epilogue by Wolfgang Volz, Skira, Milan 2001, p. 201

CHRISTO
(CHRISTO
JAVACHEFF)
Gabrovo 1935

Wrapped Monument to Vittorio Emanuele (Project for Piazza del Duomo, Milano), 1970
pencil, coloured pencil, canvas, cord, road map, photo on fibreboard
85 x 185,5 cm

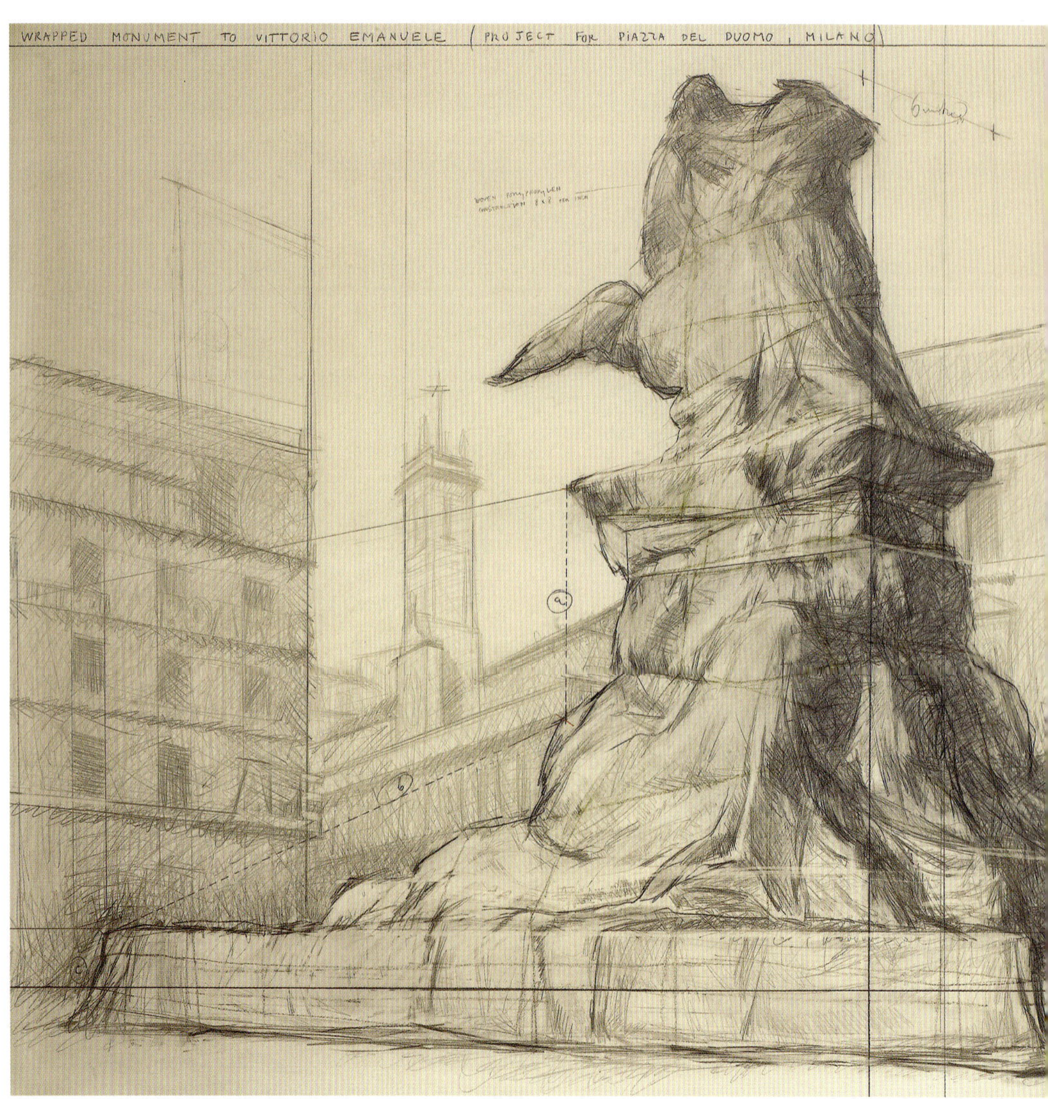

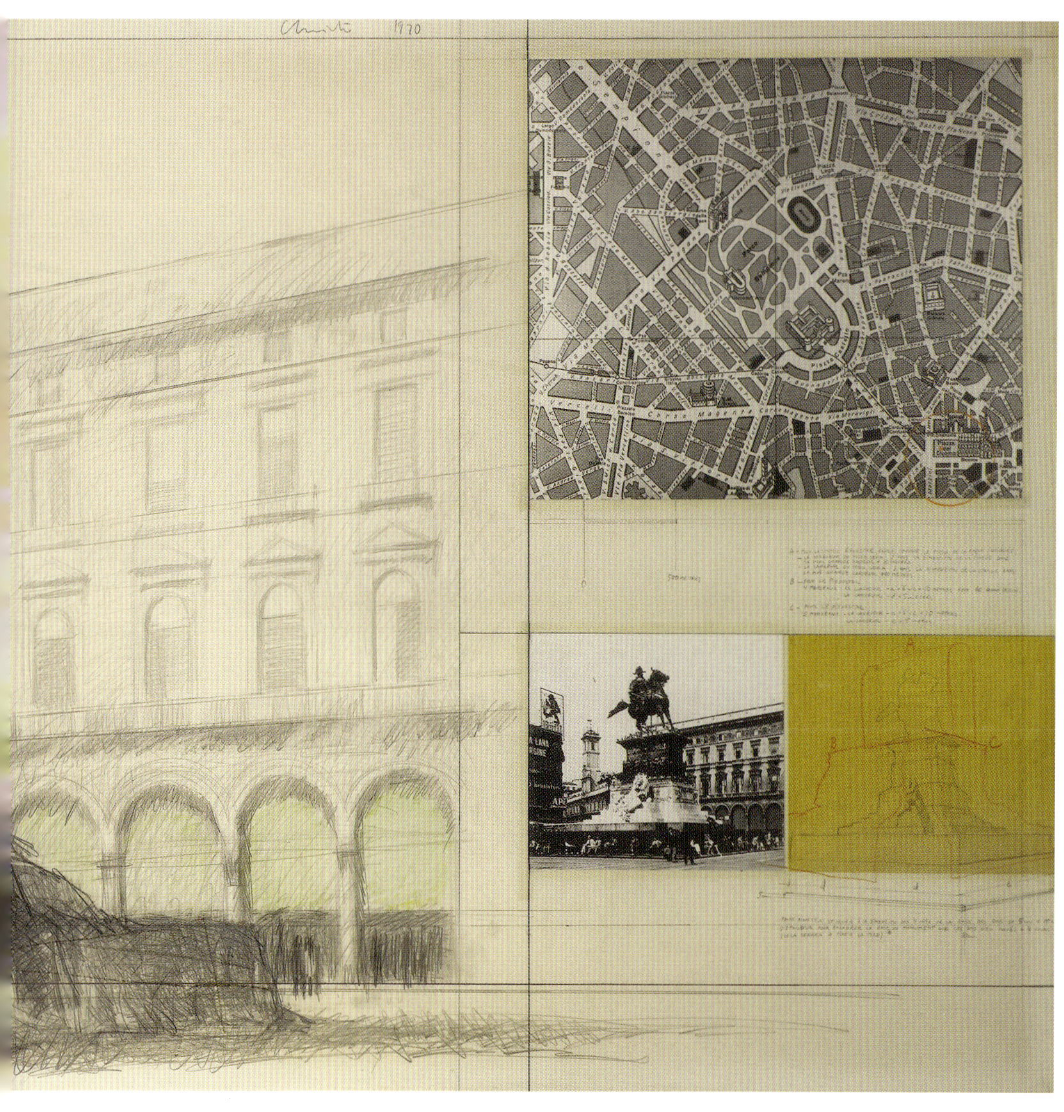

CHRISTO
(CHRISTO
JAVACHEFF)
Gabrovo 1935

*3 Wrapped Trees
(Project for P. Agrati
Park near Milan, Italy)*,
1970
pencil, coloured
pencil, canvas
on paper
71,5 x 55,9 cm

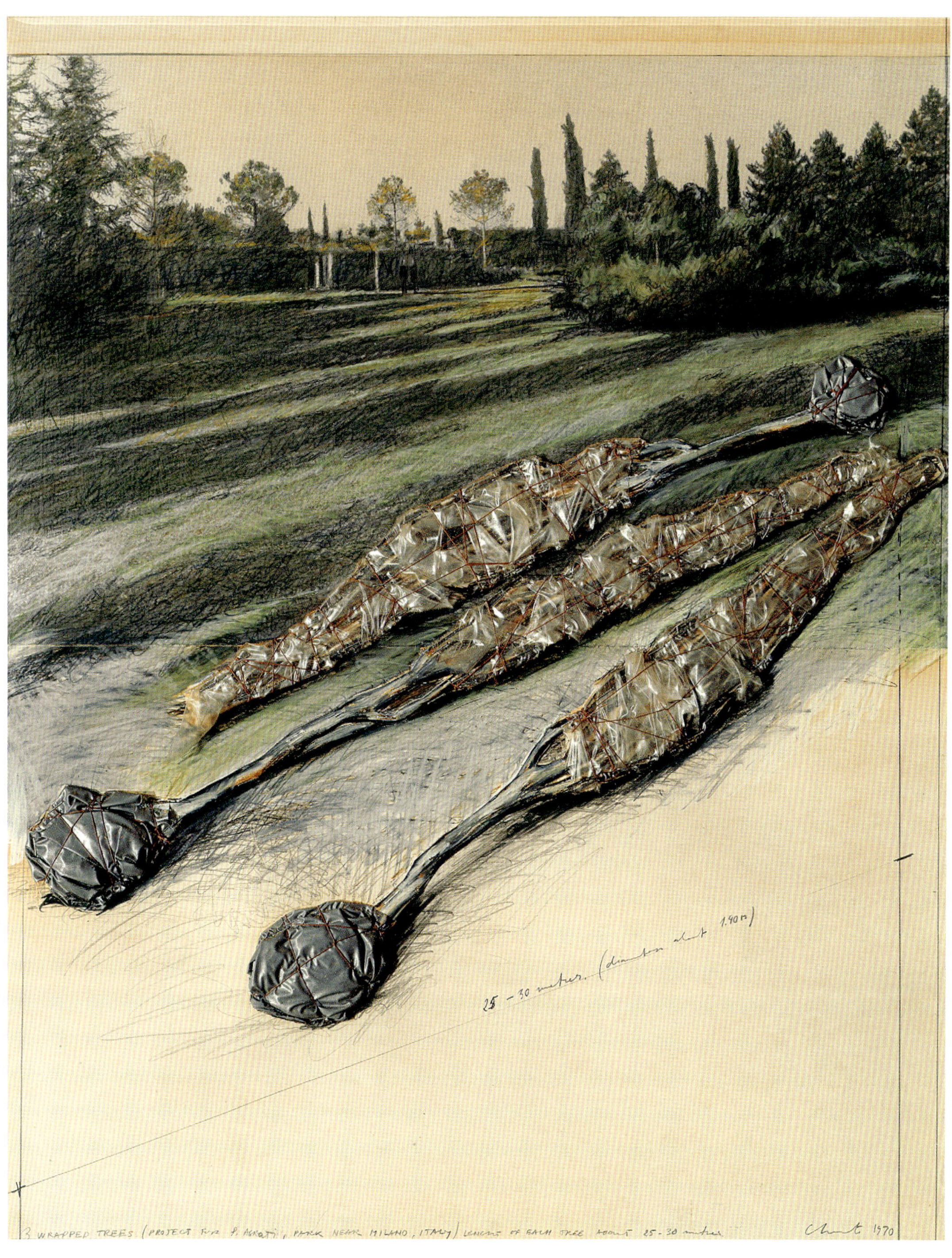
3 WRAPPED TREES (PROJECT FOR P. AGRATI, PARK NEAR MILANO, ITALY) LENGTH OF EACH TREE ABOUT 25-30
1970

CHRISTO
(CHRISTO
JAVACHEFF)
Gabrovo 1935

Curtains for the
P. Agrati's Garden,
1970
pencil, coloured
pencil, canvas
on paper
71,1 x 55,9 cm

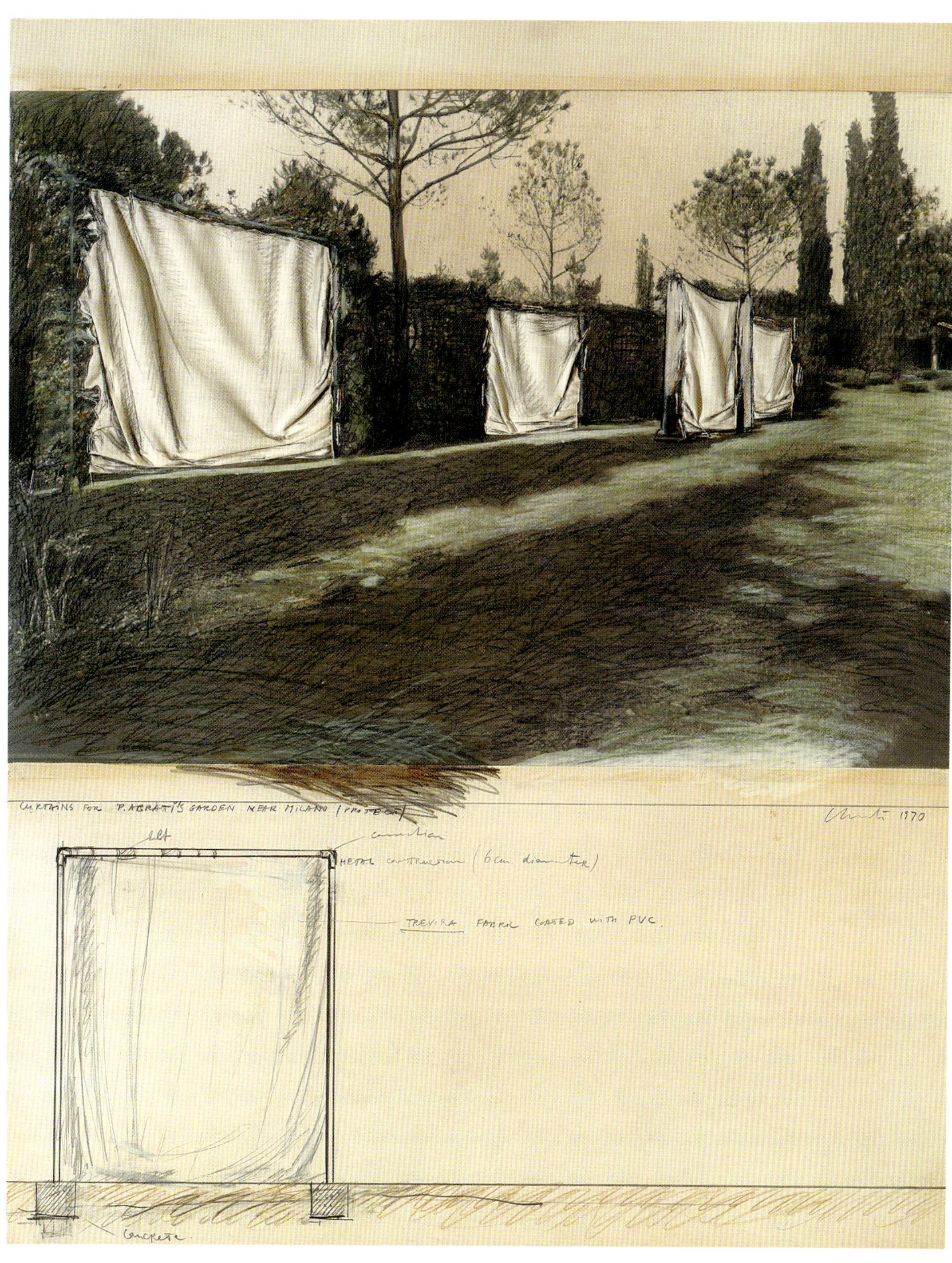
CURTAINS FOR P. ABRATI'S GARDEN NEAR MILANO (PROJECT)
1970
METAL CONSTRUCTION (6cm. diameter)
TREVIRA FABRIC COATED WITH PVC.

CHRISTO
(CHRISTO
JAVACHEFF)
Gabrovo 1935

*Curtains for the
P. Agrati's Garden
(project)*, 1970
pencil, coloured
pencil, canvas
on paper
55,9 x 71,1 cm

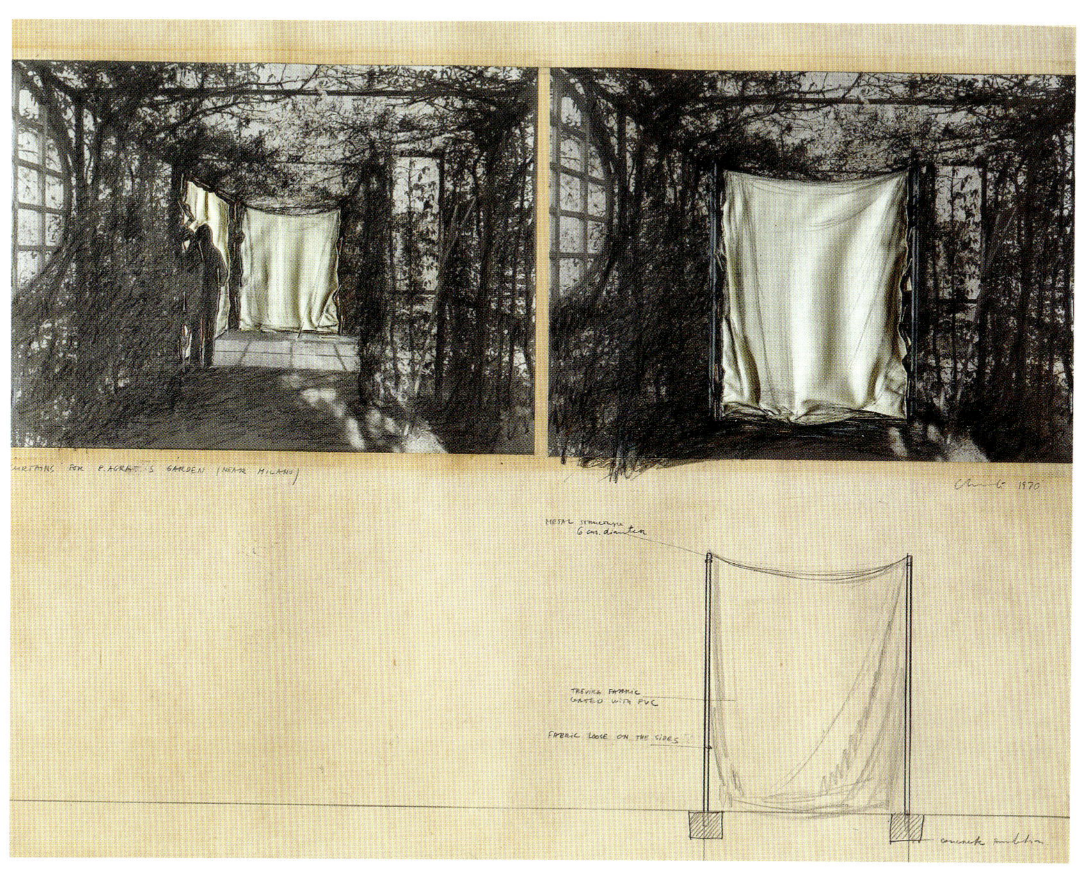

CHRISTO
(CHRISTO
JAVACHEFF)
Gabrovo 1935

Running Fence (Project for Sonoma County and Marin County, State of California), 1973
pencil on paper
90 x 244 cm

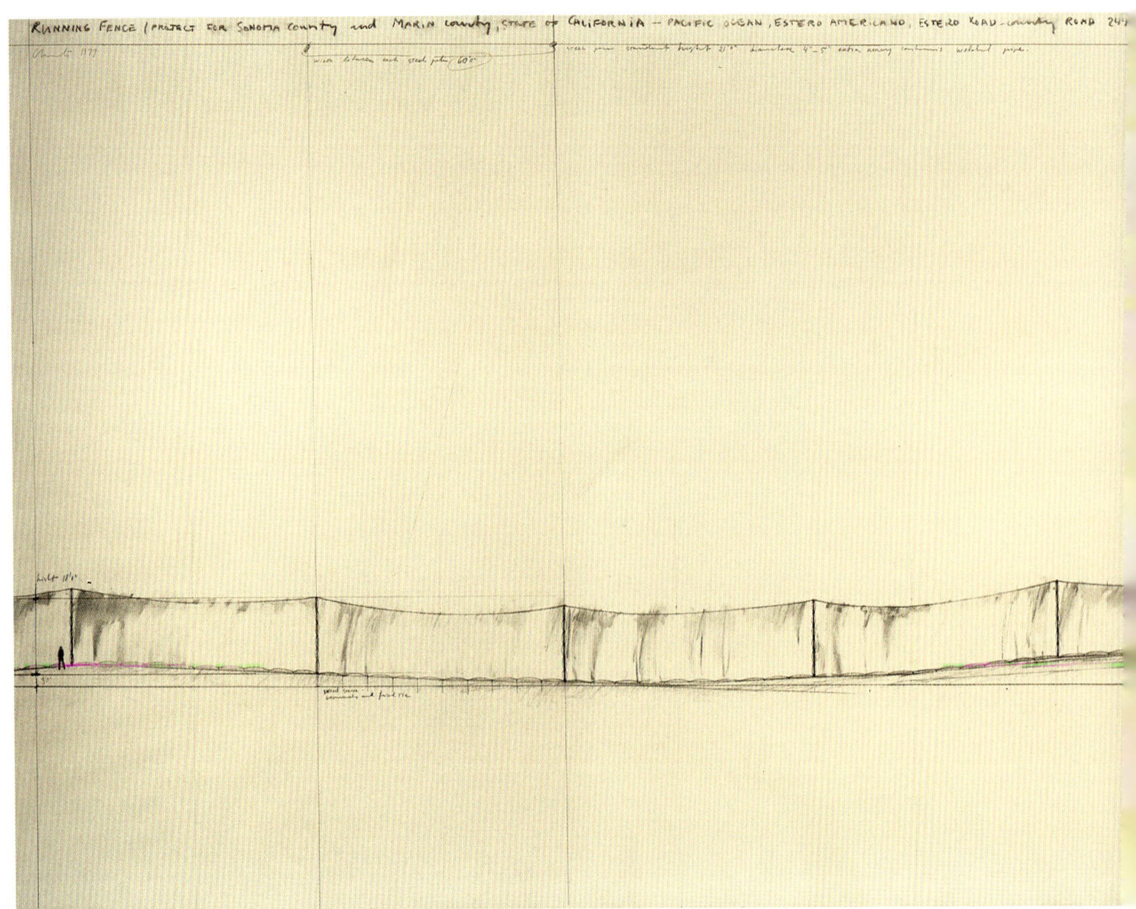

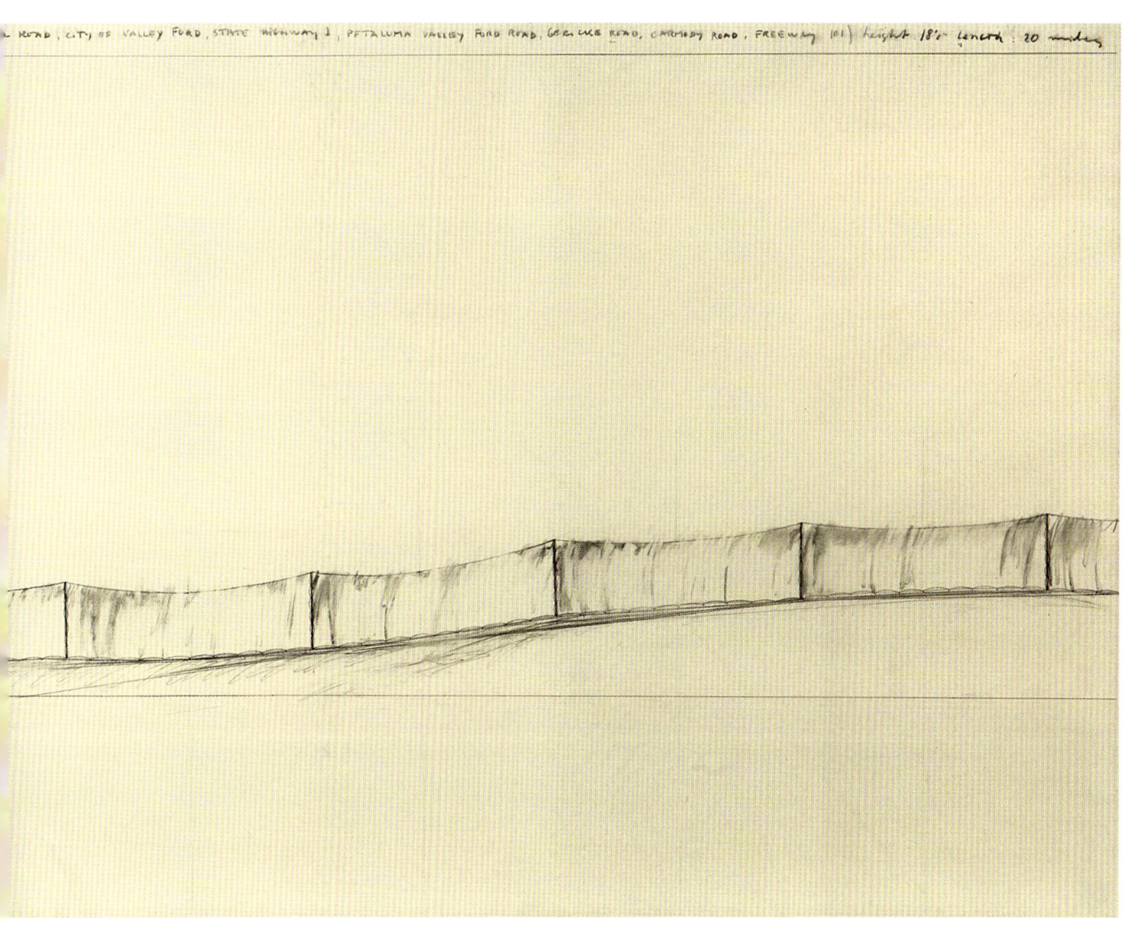
ROAD, CITY OF VALLEY FORD, STATE HIGHWAY 1, PETALUMA VALLEY FORD ROAD, GERICKE ROAD, CARMODY ROAD, FREEWAY 101) height 18' length: 20 miles

CHRISTO
(CHRISTO
JAVACHEFF)
Gabrovo 1935

Running Fence (Project for Sonoma County and Marin County, State of California), 1976

three altimetry road maps, coloured pencil on paper, drawing in two parts,
38 x 244 and 106,6 x 244 cm

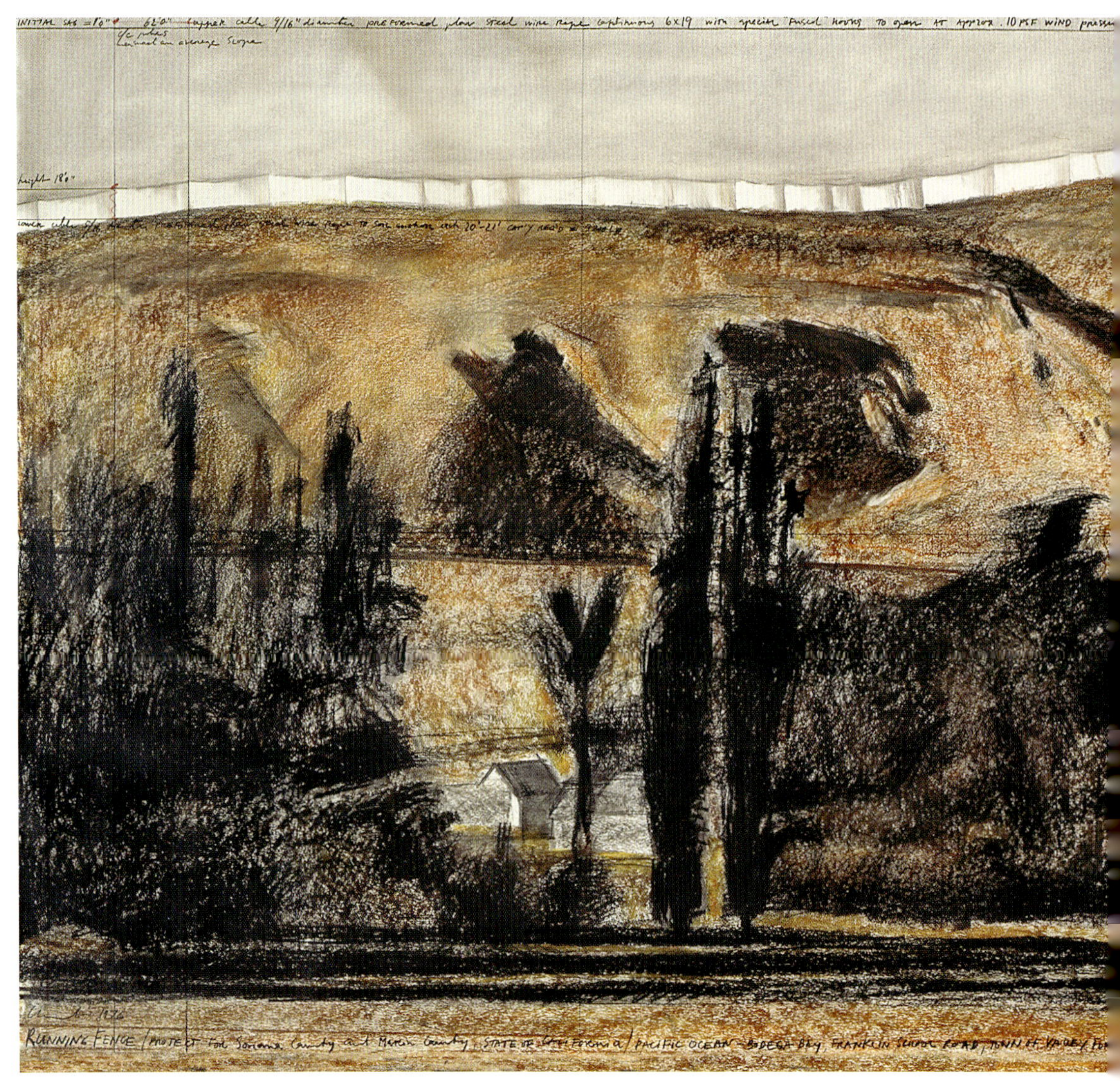

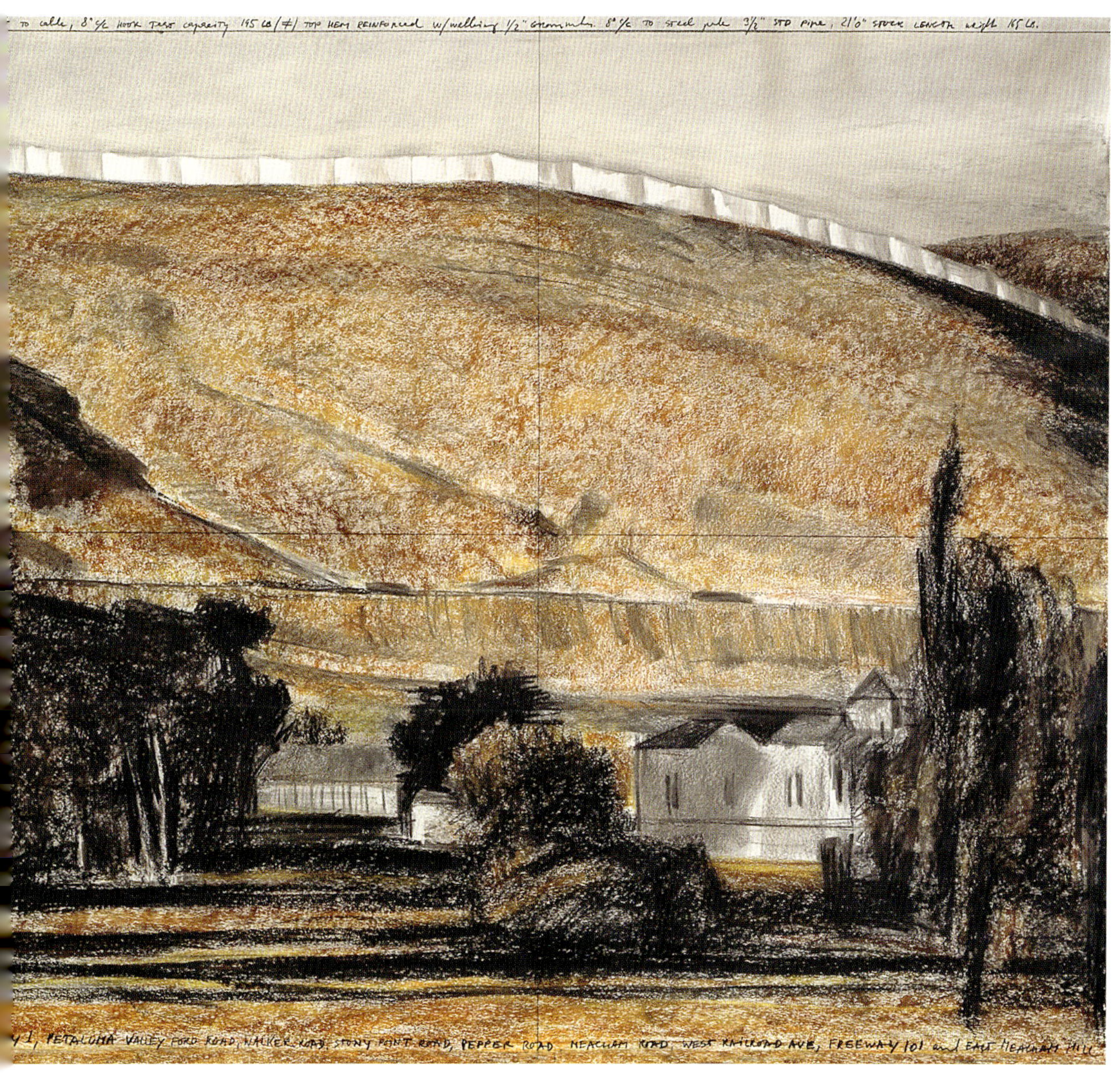
to cable, 8" o/c hook test capacity 195 lb (#) top hem reinforced w/webbing 1/2" grommets. 8" o/c to steel pole 3 1/2" std pipe, 21'0" stock length weight 165 lb.
y 1, PETALUMA VALLEY FORD ROAD, WALKER ROAD, STONY POINT ROAD, PEPPER ROAD MEACHAM ROAD WEST RAILROAD AVE, FREEWAY 101 and EAST MEACHAM HILL

CHRISTO
(CHRISTO
JAVACHEFF)
Gabrovo 1935

Running Fence
(Sonoma County), 1976
crayon, pencil,
coloured pencil,
mixed media on paper
106,5 x 242,5 cm

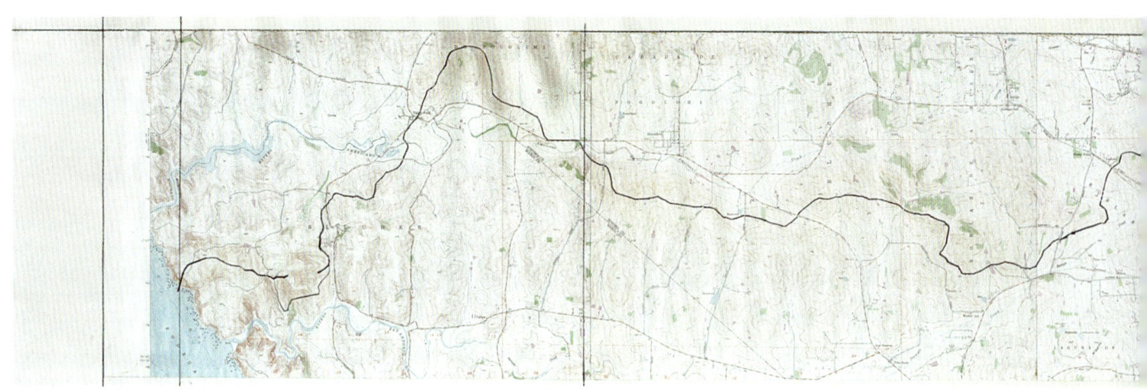

Sonoma County – PETALUMA INVESTMENT ASS – Karen and Francis WATSON 118-150-01

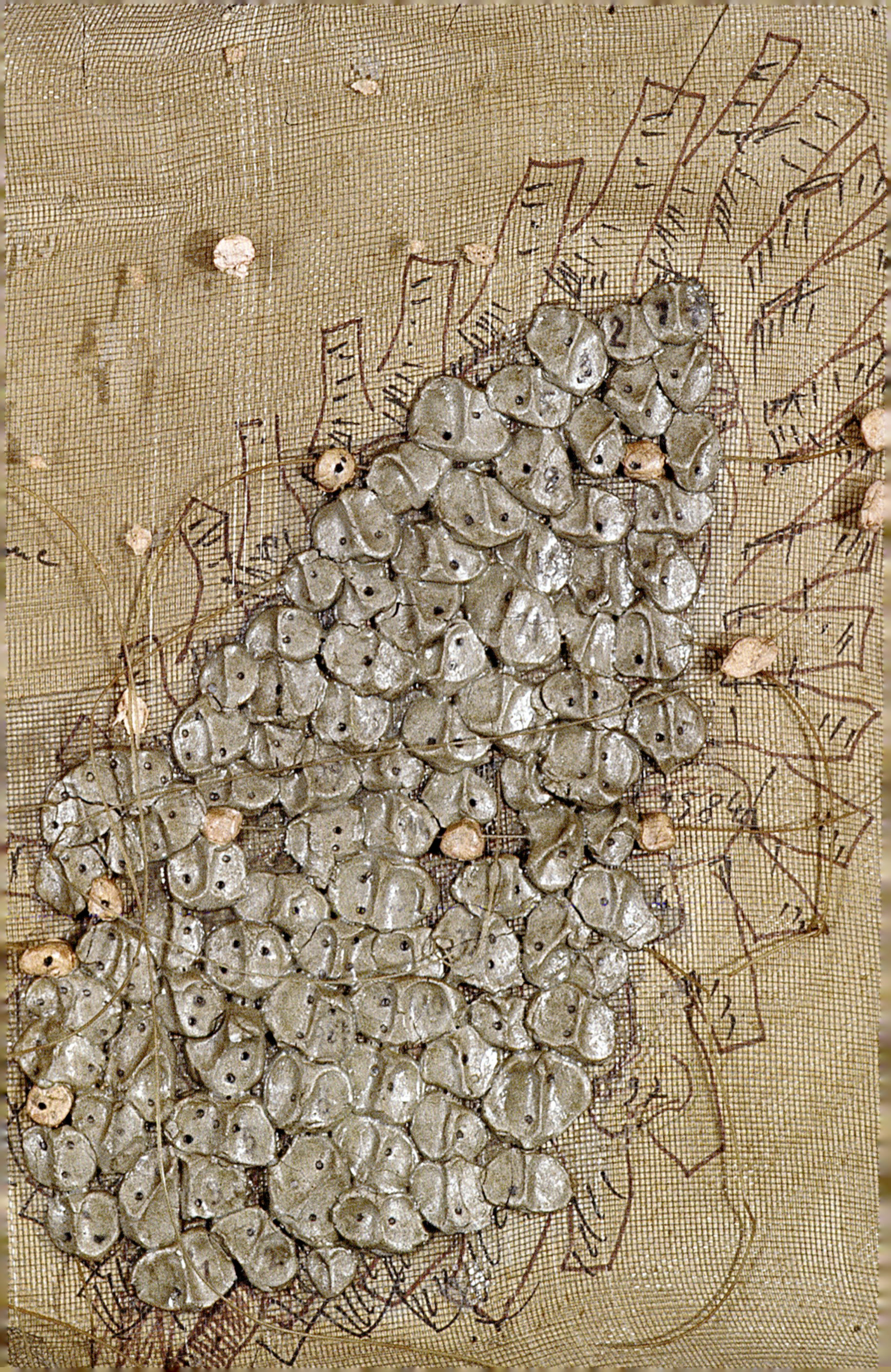

FROM NATURE TO ART

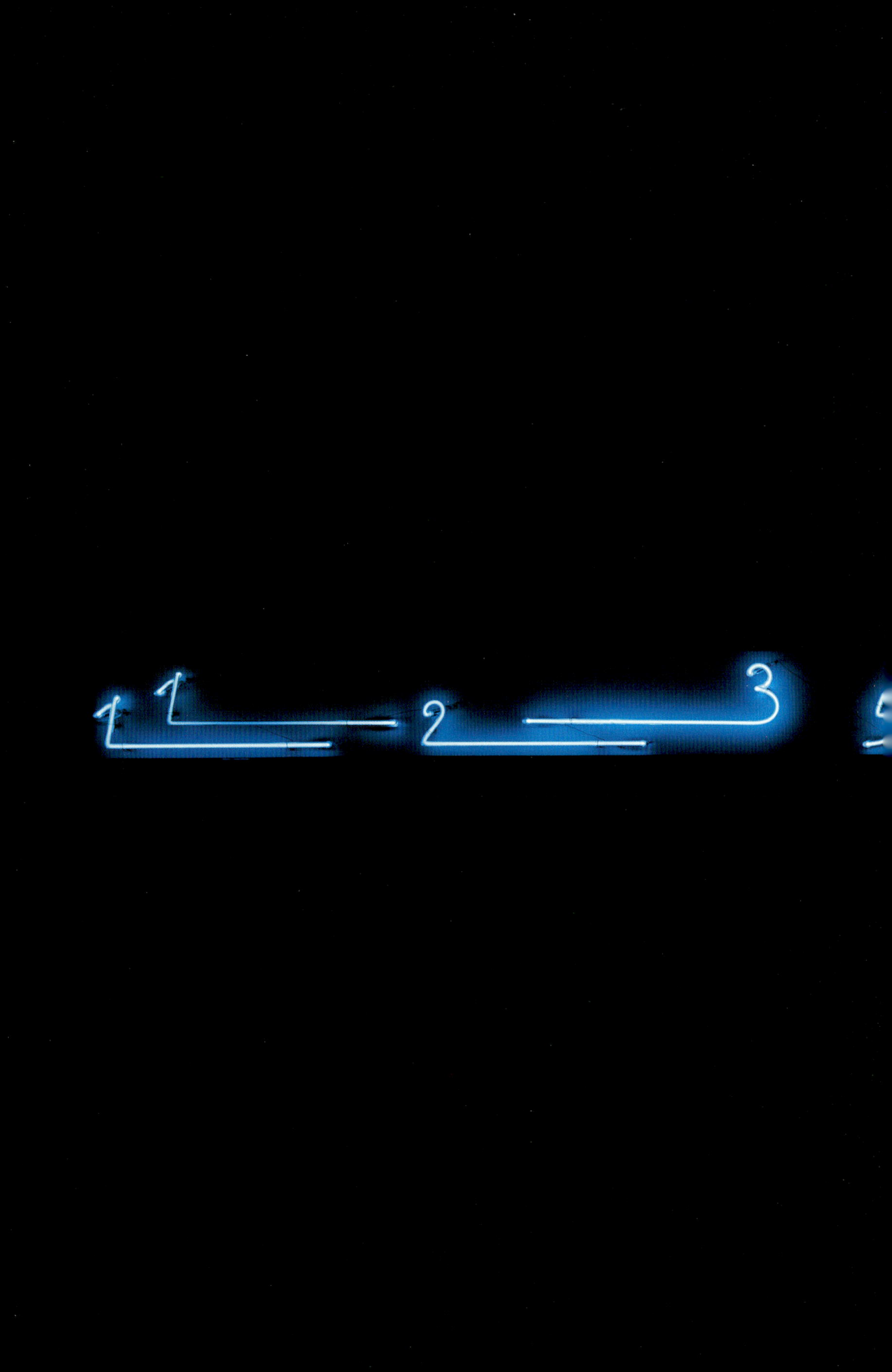

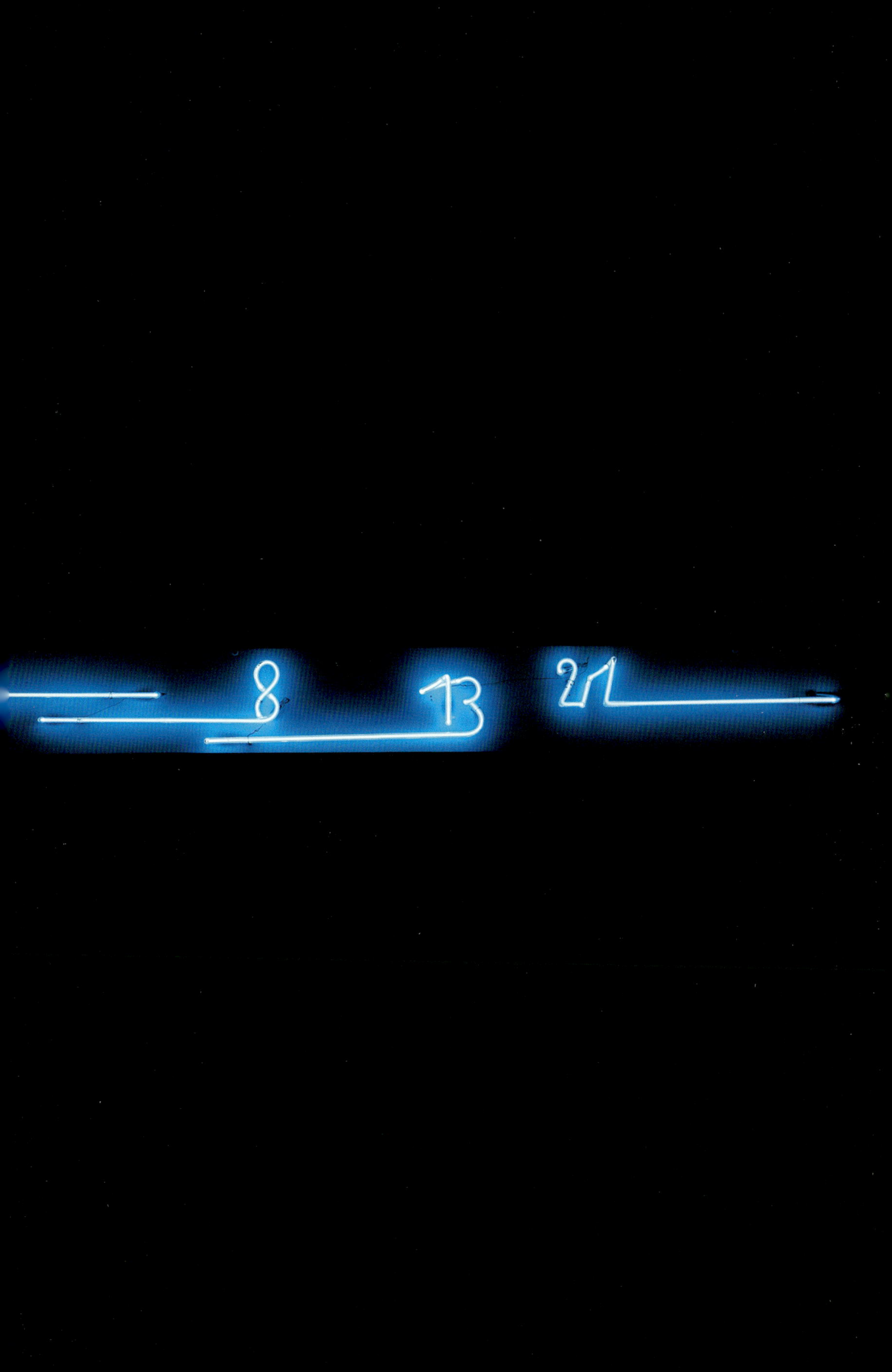

on the previous pages

MARIO MERZ
Milan 1925 – Turin 2003

Plant Proliferation,
1970
neon numbers

"ANIMALS, VEGETABLES AND MINERALS TAKE PART IN THE WORLD OF ART. THE ARTIST FEELS ATTRACTED BY THEIR PHYSICAL, CHEMICAL AND BIOLOGICAL POSSIBILITIES, AND HE BEGINS AGAIN TO FEEL THE NEED TO MAKE THINGS OF THE WORLD, NOT ONLY AS ANIMATED BEINGS, BUT AS A PRODUCER OF MAGIC AND MARVELOUS DEEDS. THE ARTIST-ALCHEMIST ORGANISES LIVING AND VEGETABLE MATTER INTO MAGIC THINGS, WORKING TO DISCOVER THE ROOT OF THINGS, IN ORDER TO RE-FIND THEM AND EXTOL THEM."

GERMANO CELANT
Arte Povera, Mazzotta, Milan 1969

MARIO MERZ
Milan 1925 – Turin 2003

Senza titolo [Untitled],
1968
black felt-pen,
metallic mesh, clay,
oil, paper on board
54 x 73 cm

Le api maschio si riproducono
secondo la teoria di Fibonacci,
e si è constatato che il numero
delle formazioni di flosculi a
spirale, visibili in molti girasoli
le scaglie a spirale di una pigna
e i segmenti sulla superficie
di un ananasso si uniformano
ai numeri di Fibonacci - il disegno
dei rami di molti alberi, la posizione
delle foglie sui rami stessi e la formazione
dei petali di gran parte dei fiori
vengono più descritti per mezzo di
numeri della serie di Fibonacci.
Il LIBER ABACI è pubblicato
a Pisa nell'anno 1202 -

PIERO GILARDI
Turin 1942

Senza titolo [Untitled],
undated
polyurethane foam,
ten elements

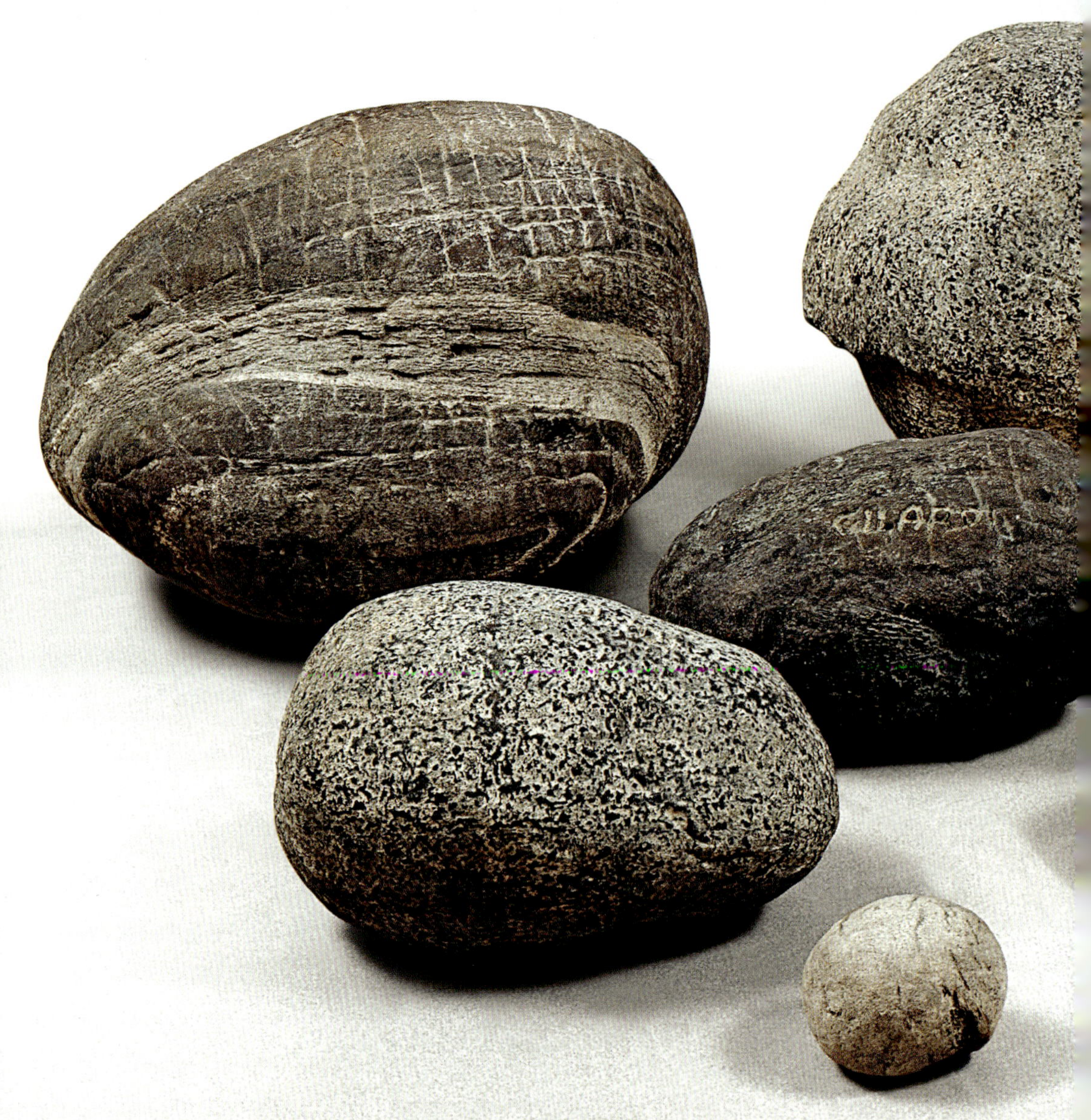

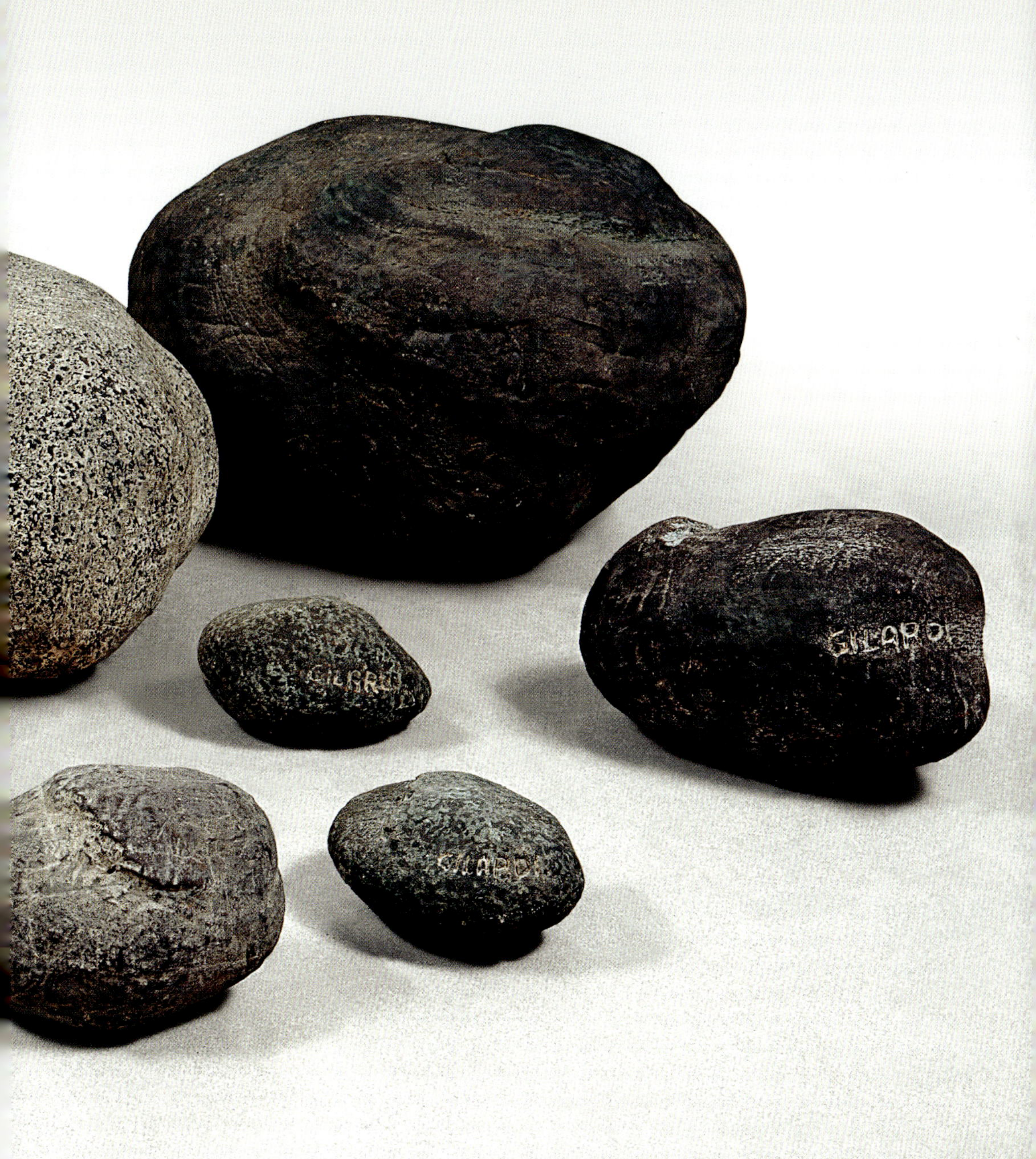

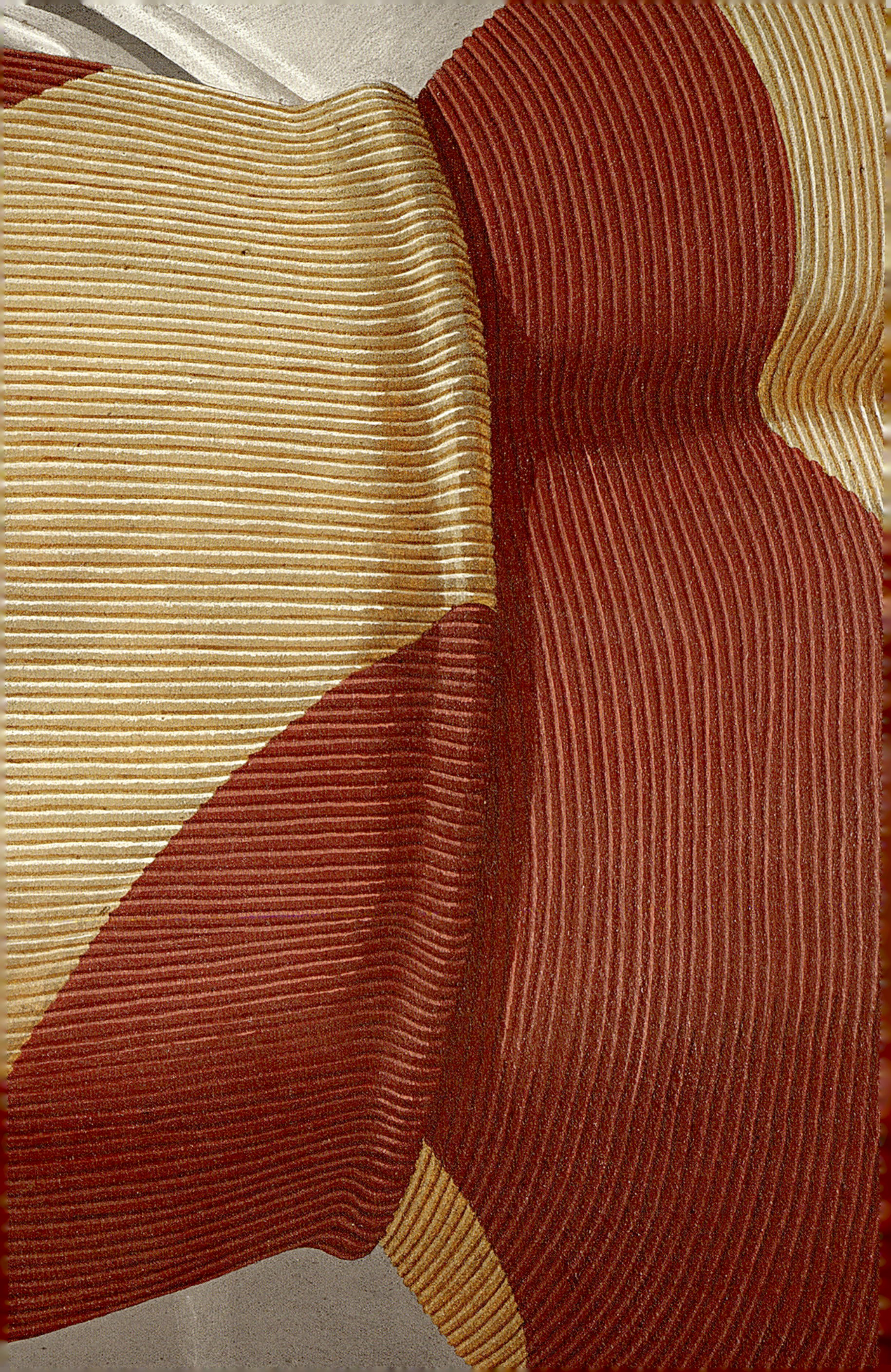

ITALY IN THE SIXTIES:
ART BETWEEN IMAGE AND CONCEPT

I'M A METAPHYSICAL ARTIST INSOFAR AS I SEEK A NON-ELOQUENT, MOTIONLESS PAINTING, FULL OF ATMOSPHERE AND FEEDING ON STATIC SITUATIONS. I'M *NOT* A METAPHYSICAL ARTIST BECAUSE I'VE NEVER ATTEMPTED TO STAGE OR MANUFACTURE AN IMAGE. I USE SIMPLE, GIVEN ELEMENTS; I DON'T WANT TO ADD OR SUBTRACT ANYTHING. I'VE NEVER EVEN WANTED TO DEFORM: INSTEAD, I ISOLATE AND REPRESENT.
MY MOTIFS STEM FROM CURRENT EVENTS, FROM THE FAMILIAR SITUATIONS OF DAILY LIFE; SINCE I NEVER ACTIVELY INTERFERE WITH AN OBJECT, I CAN SENSE THE MAGIC UNDERLYING ITS PRESENCE. [...] I DON'T THINK IMAGINATION AND INVENTION CAN CREATE ANYTHING MORE IMPORTANT – MORE BEAUTIFUL AND TERRIBLE – THAN AN EVERYDAY OBJECT, MAGNIFIED BY THE ATTENTION WE BESTOW ON IT. IT SPEAKS MORE OF ME THAN ANYTHING ELSE, IT FILLS ME WITH FEAR, WITH DISGUST AND ENCHANTMENT.

DOMENICO GNOLI

In Jean-Luc Daval, *Artitude-Interview*, in "Le Journal de Genève", Geneva, 5th June 1965

DOMENICO GNOLI
Rome 1933 – New York 1970

Bow tie, 1969
acrylic and sand
on canvas
140 x 160 cm

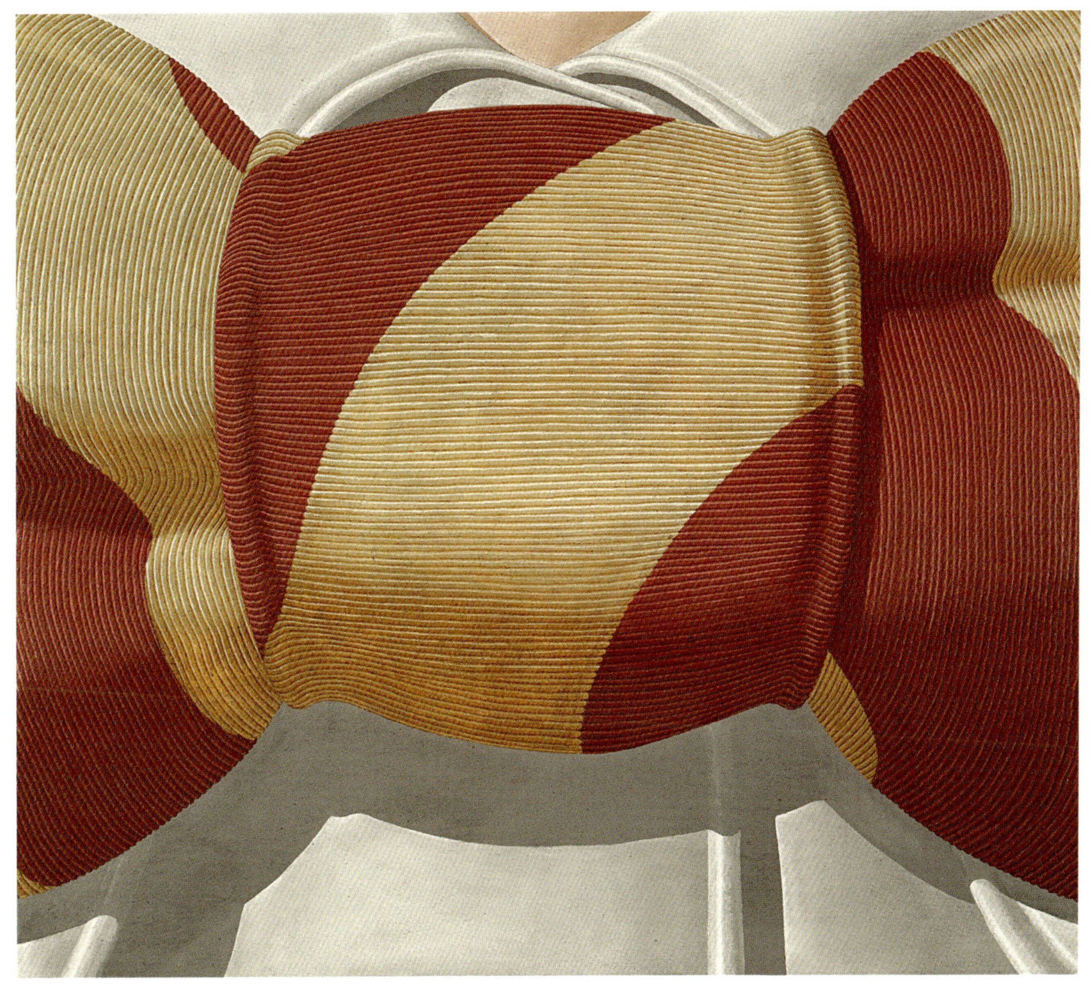

IN MARCH 1962 AT THE PROMOTRICE IN TURIN I EXHIBITED MY FIRST MIRROR-PAINTING, ENTITLED THE PRESENT. THE FIGURE OF A MAN SEEMED TO COME FORWARD, AS IF ALIVE, IN THE SPACE OF THE GALLERY; BUT THE TRUE PROTAGONIST WAS THE RELATIONSHIP OF INSTANTANEOUSNESS WHICH WAS CREATED BETWEEN THE SPECTATOR, HIS OWN REFLECTION, AND THE PAINTED FIGURE, IN AN EVER-PRESENT MOVEMENT WHICH CONCENTRATED THE PAST AND THE FUTURE IN ITSELF TO SUCH AN EXTENT AS TO CAUSE ONE TO CALL THEIR VERY EXISTENCE INTO DOUBT: IT WAS THE DIMENSION OF TIME ITSELF.

MICHELANGELO PISTOLETTO

Oggetti in meno, in *Michelangelo Pistoletto*, exhibition catalogue,
(Genoa, Galleria La Bertesca, December 1966 - January 1967), Genoa 1966

MICHELANGELO
PISTOLETTO
Biella 1933

Uomo che aggiusta un camion [Man Repairing a Van], 1967
painted tissue paper,
polished mirror-finish
stainless steel
230 x 120 cm

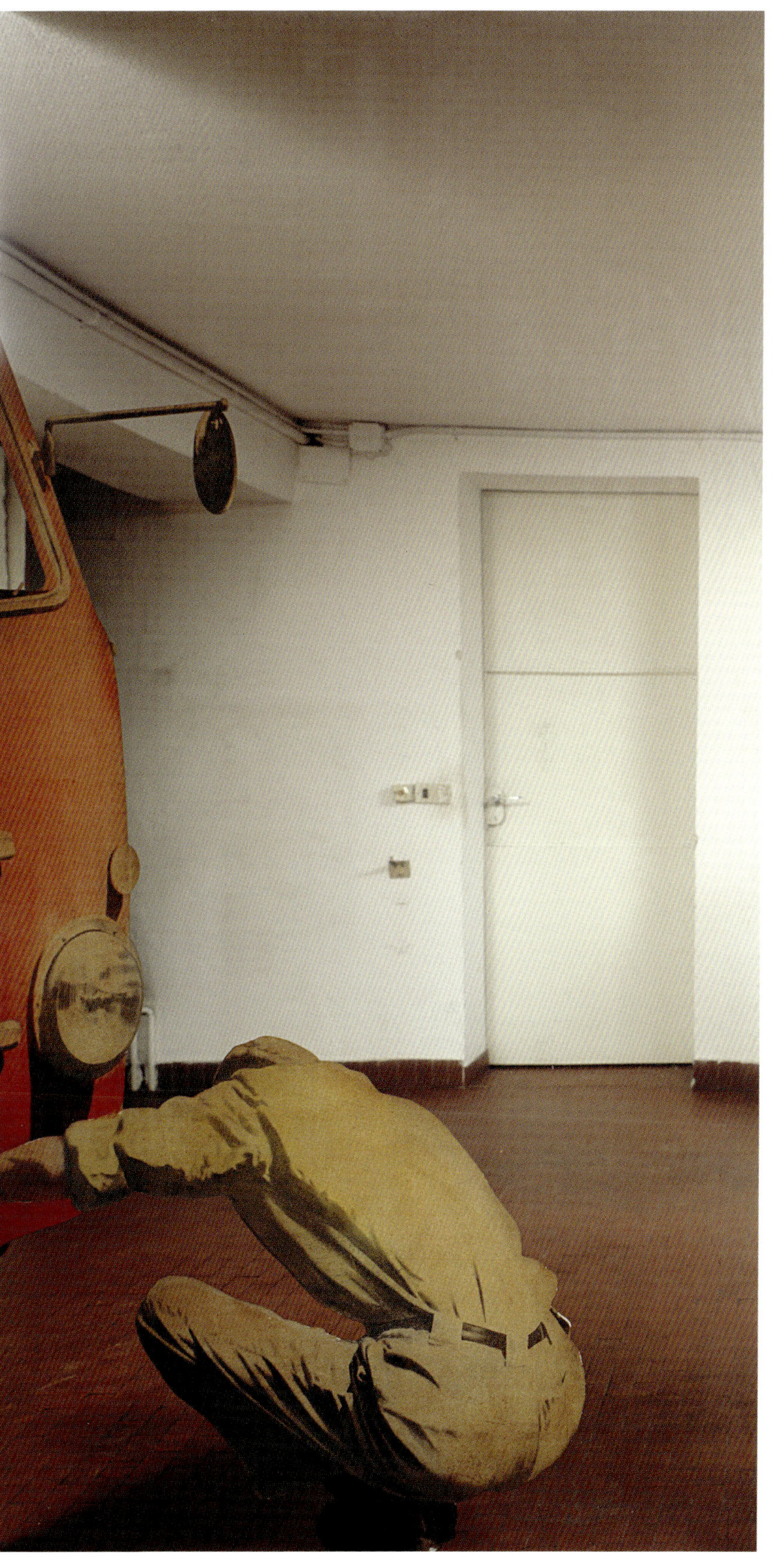

on the following pages

ALIGHIERO BOETTI
Turin 1940 – Rome 1994

I vedenti [Those Who See], 1973
hand embroidery
on linen
167 x 141 cm

I vedenti [Those Who See], 1973
hand embroidery
on linen
166 x 133 cm

ALIGHIERO BOETTI
Turin 1940 – Rome 1994

I vedenti [Those Who See], 1973
hand embroidery
on linen
155 x 161,5 cm

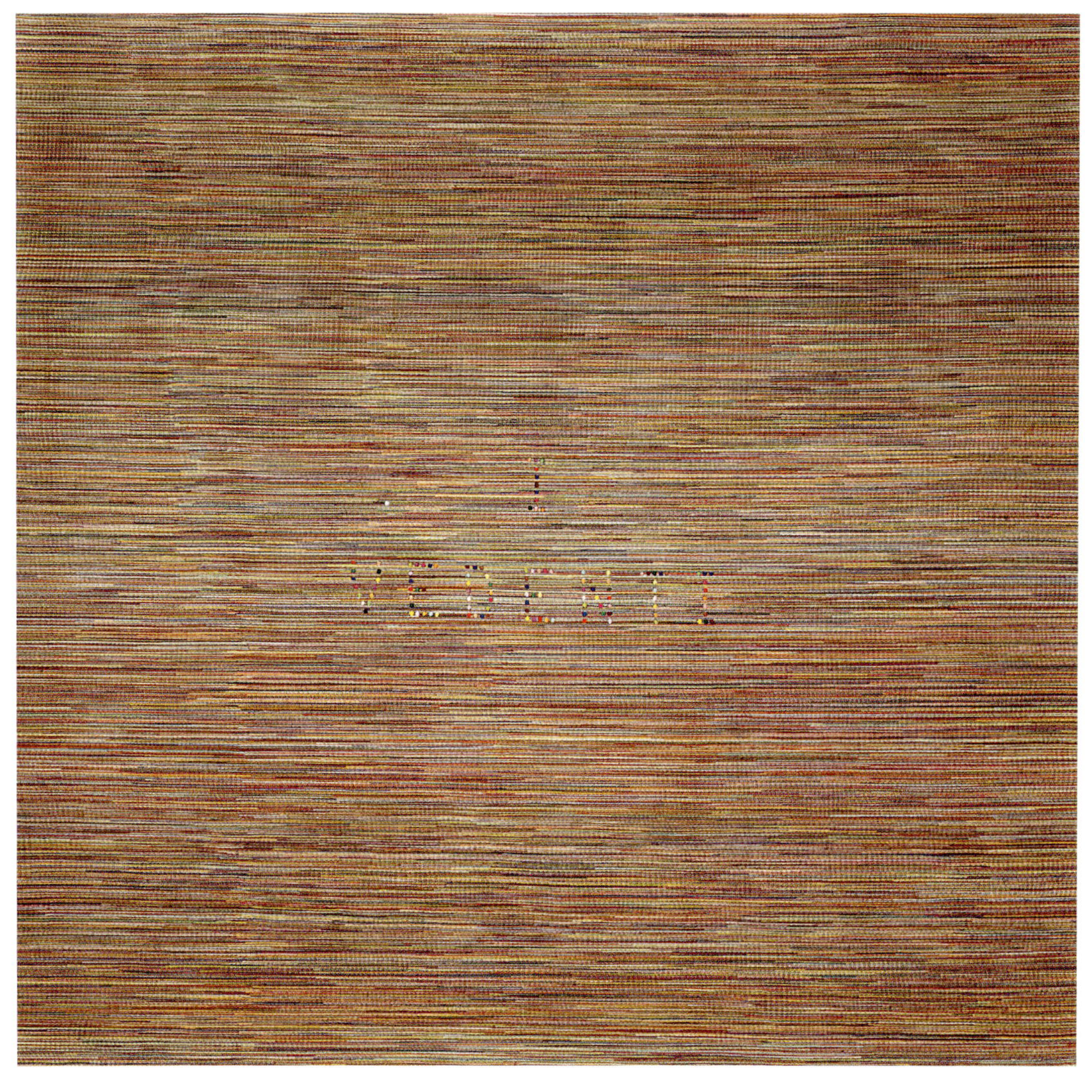

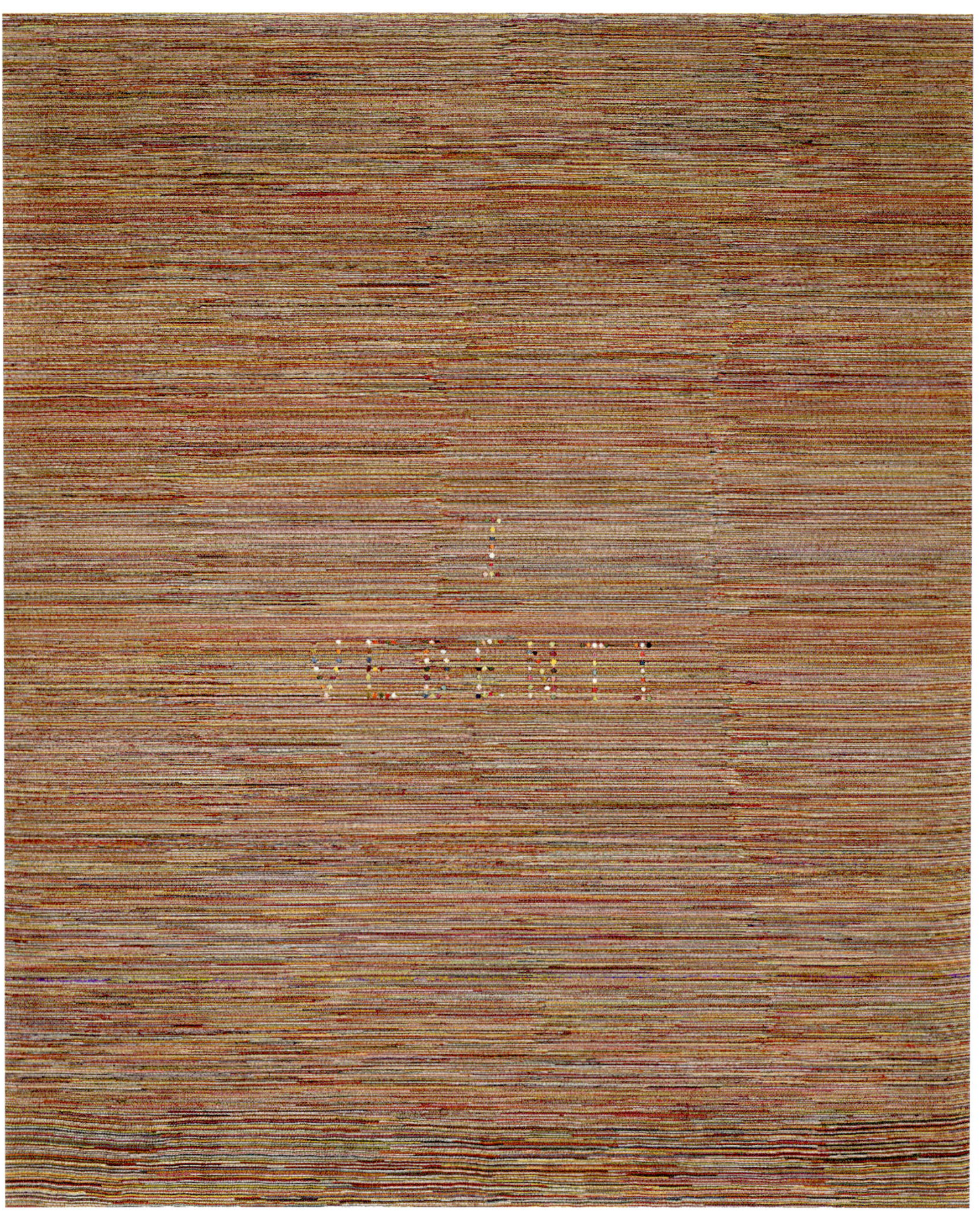

ALIGHIERO BOETTI
Turin 1940 - Rome 1994

I vedenti [Those Who See], 1973
hand embroidery
on linen
164,5 x 140 cm

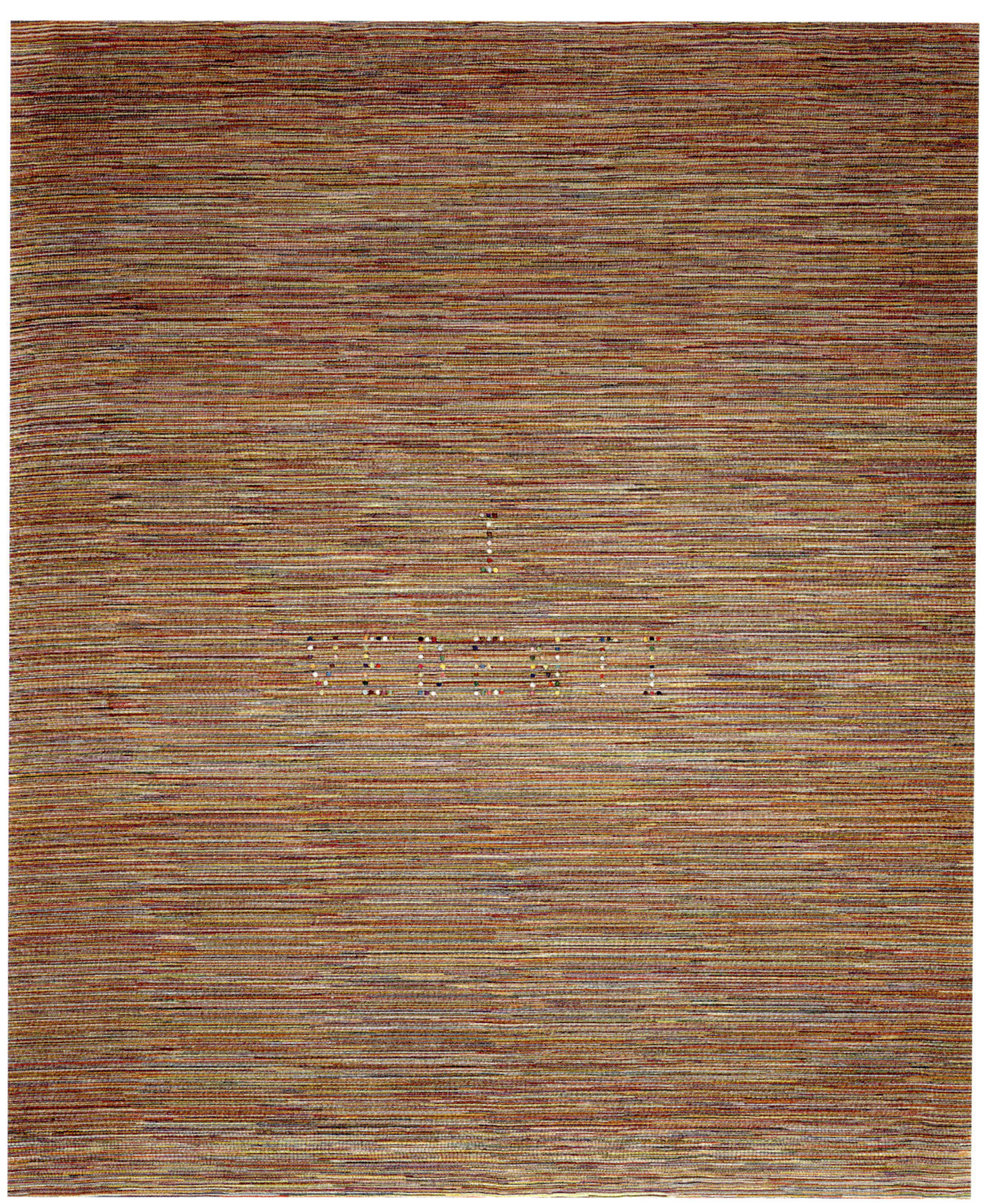

MARIO SCHIFANO
Homs 1934 – Rome 1998

Grande pittura [Great Painting], 1963
enamel and graphite on paper applied onto canvas
260 x 150 cm

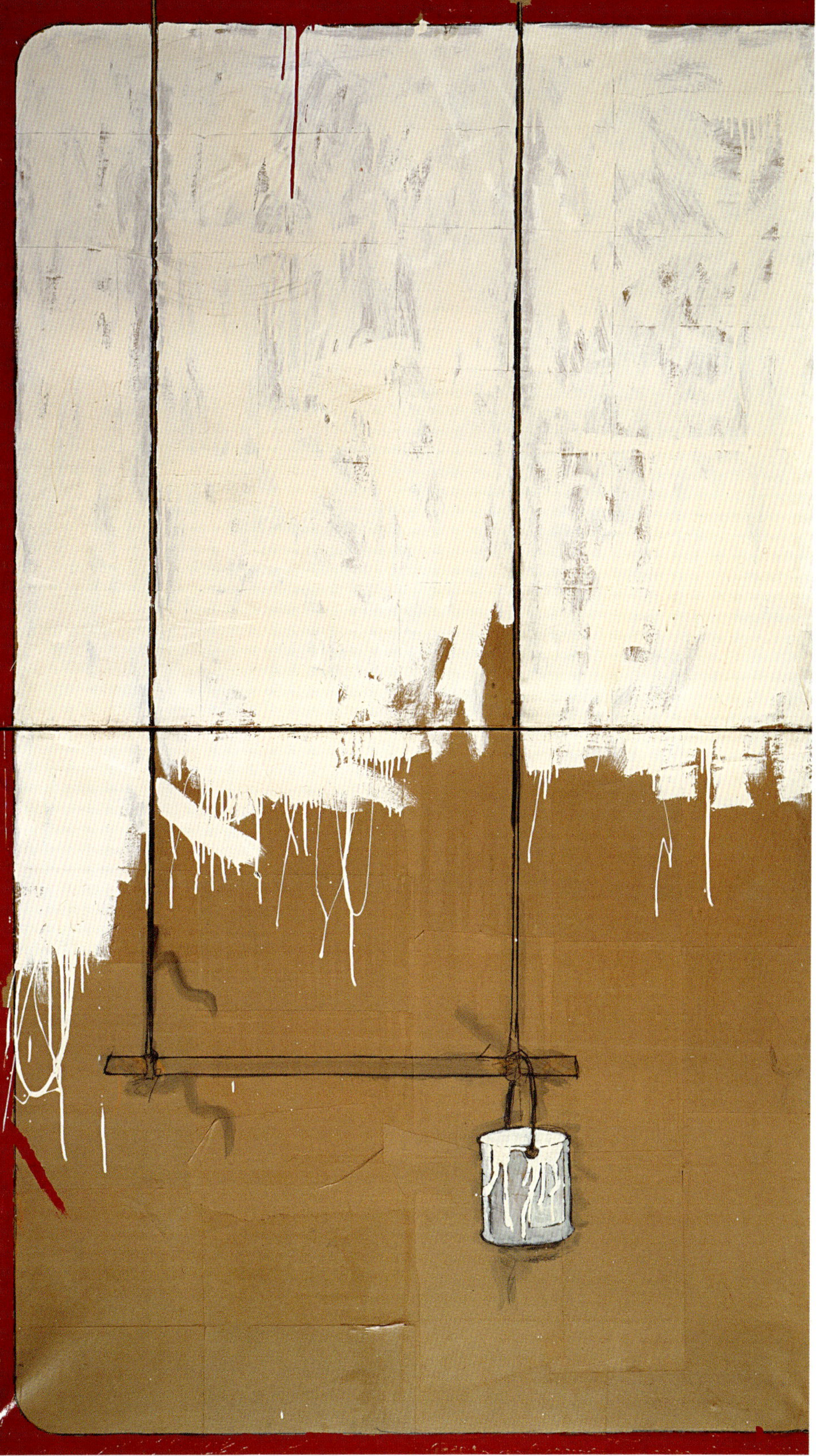

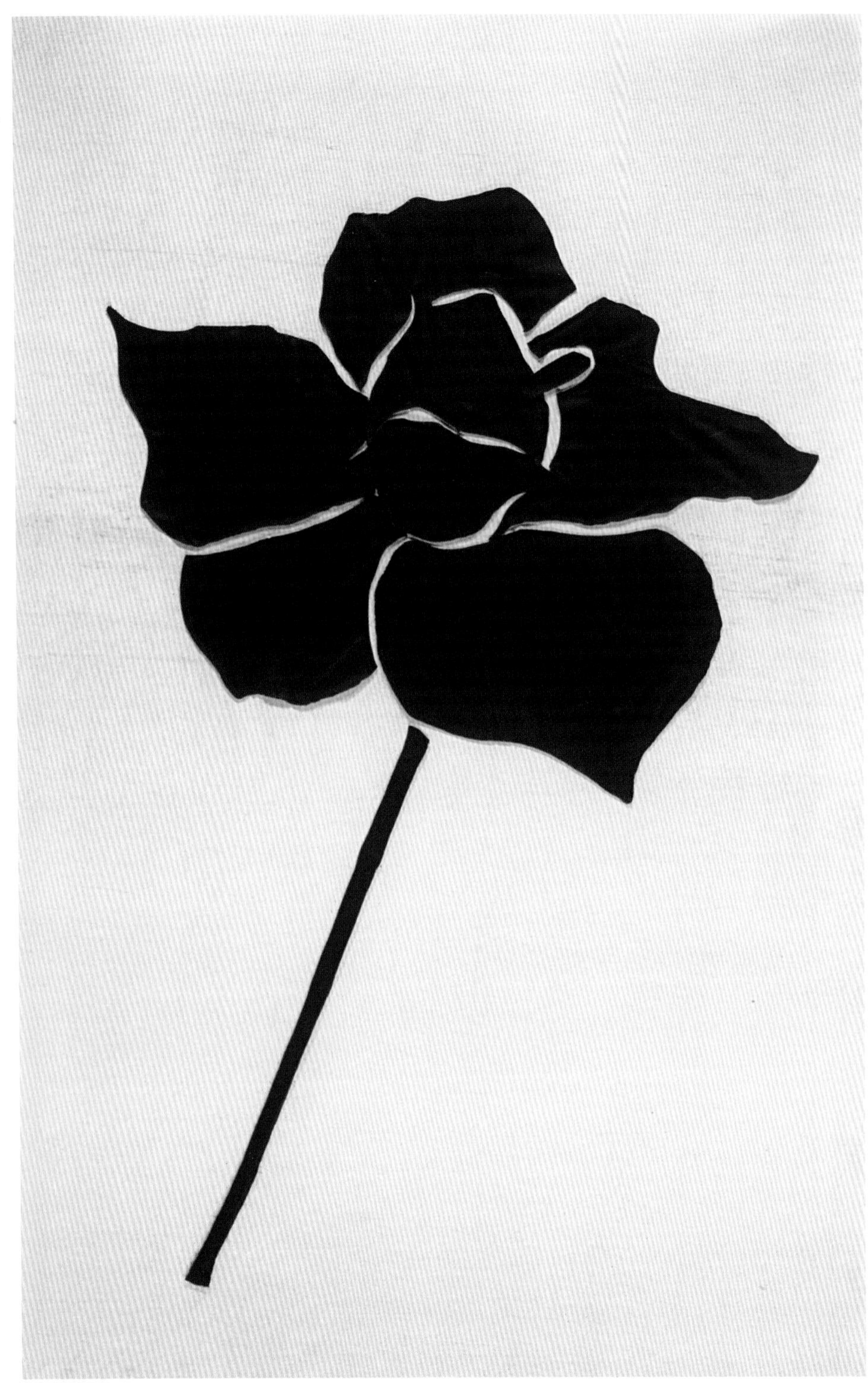

JOINT INDUSTRIAL WRITING" AS ROAD SIGNS; DIRECTIONAL, ARITHMETIC, CULTURAL SYMBOLS (I.E., THE SWASTIKA – A SYMBOL OF WAR FOR WOTAN, OF MYSTICISM FOR BUDDHA, OF RAVAGING FOR HITLER); SQUARES AND CIRCLES, CHESSBOARDS, PROHIBITION NOTICES AND PASSABLE ROADS. IF YOU TAKE A STEP WESTWARDS, A MENTAL ARROW DRAWS YOU TOWARDS THE EAST, BUT THE MULTIPLYING SIGN ESTABLISHES A PROHIBITION, AND FREEDOM TURNS TOWARDS THE DIRTY SOUTHERN DESERT.
THE GRAPHIC EPOS OF A CITY SEIZED FROM THE ORDINARY EVERYDAY LIFE WHEREIN MYTHOLOGICAL ARCHETYPES HAVE BEEN REDISCOVERED, AND USED AS ALPHABET, NOMENCLATURE, DICTIONARY, PENAL MAZE, VISUAL OBJECT, HALLUCINATION CONTENT, FIGURATIVE REPORT ON THE STATUS OF PAINTING, SOLVER OF CONFLICTS – BETWEEN INDIVIDUAL AND MATTER, BETWEEN SURFACE, SPACE AND MEANINGFUL OBJECTS. A REALISTIC – THAT IS, METAPHYSICAL, TALE – IDEAS IN MOTION AND DENIED PHYSICAL MOTION, PSYCHIC WALKWAY, NERVOUS INTEGRATION, VISIONARY REPRODUCTION OF THE TRUTH.

MARIO DIACONO

L'alfabeto di Kounellis, in "Catalogo 1 - La Tartaruga", Rome, February 1961

JANNIS
KOUNELLIS
Piraeus 1936 – Rome 2017

Senza titolo (Rose) [Untitled (Rose)], 1967
cotton, canvas, press studs
199,5 x 129,5 cm

on the previous pages

JANNIS
KOUNELLIS
Piraeus 1936 – Rome 2017

Senza titolo [Untitled], 1960
oil on canvas
150 x 250 cm

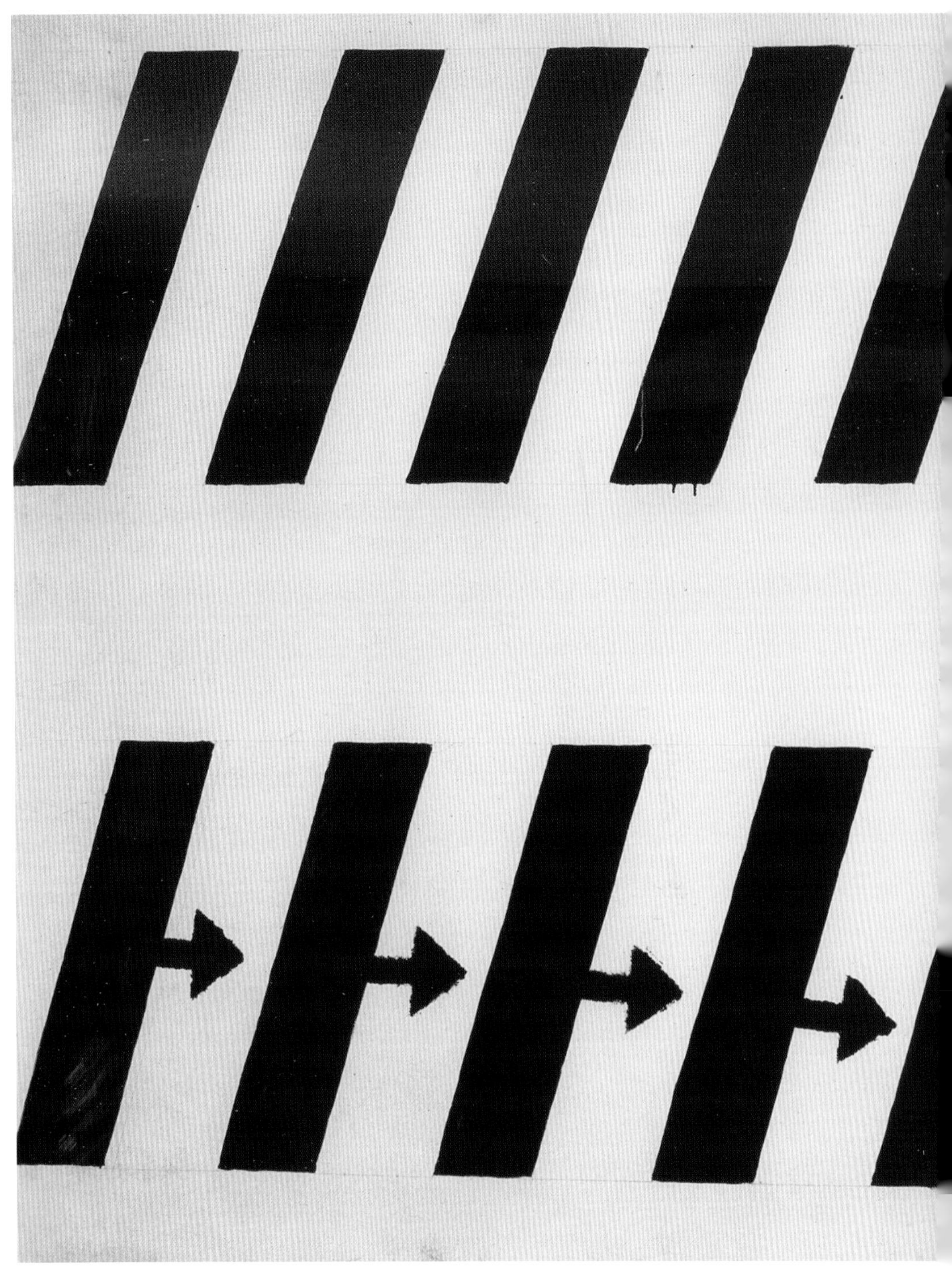

PINO PASCALI
Polignano a Mare 1935 –
Rome 1968

Ricostruzione della balena [Reconstruction of the Whale], 1966
canvas stretched over wooden frame
100 x 366 x 90 cm

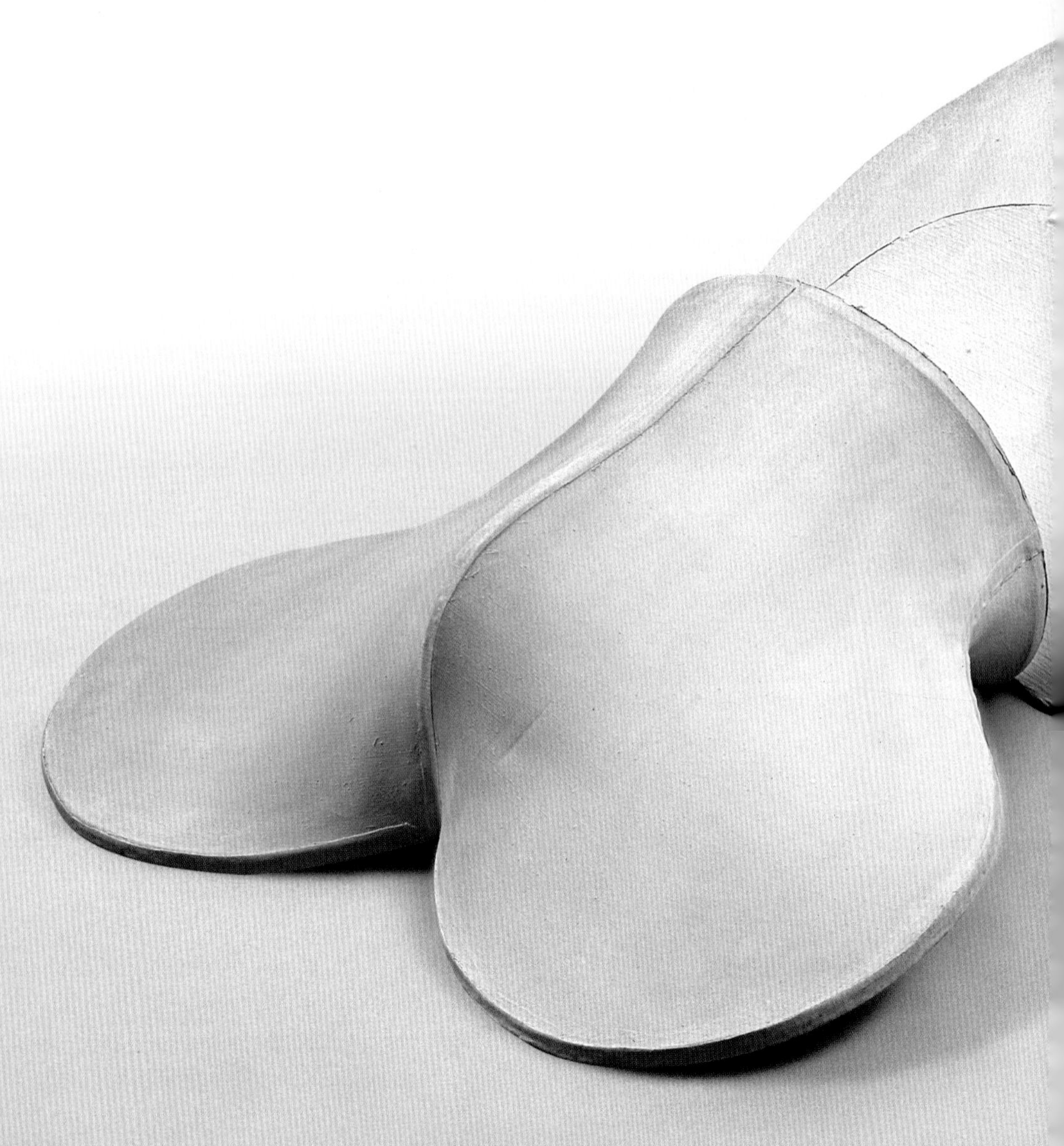

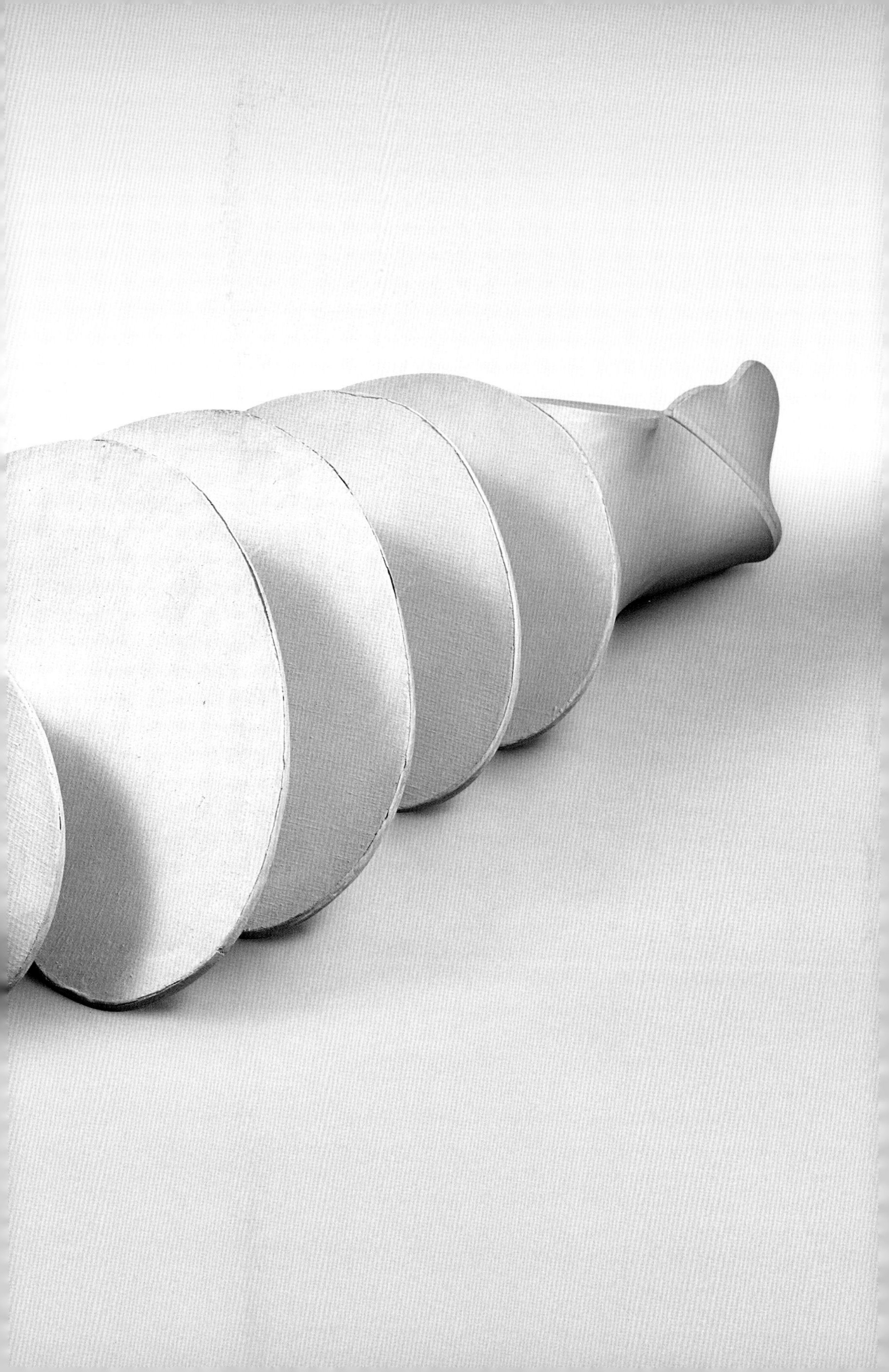

GIULIO PAOLINI
Genoa 1940

Senza titolo [Untitled], 1961
jute, polythene, cord, frame
120 x 150 cm

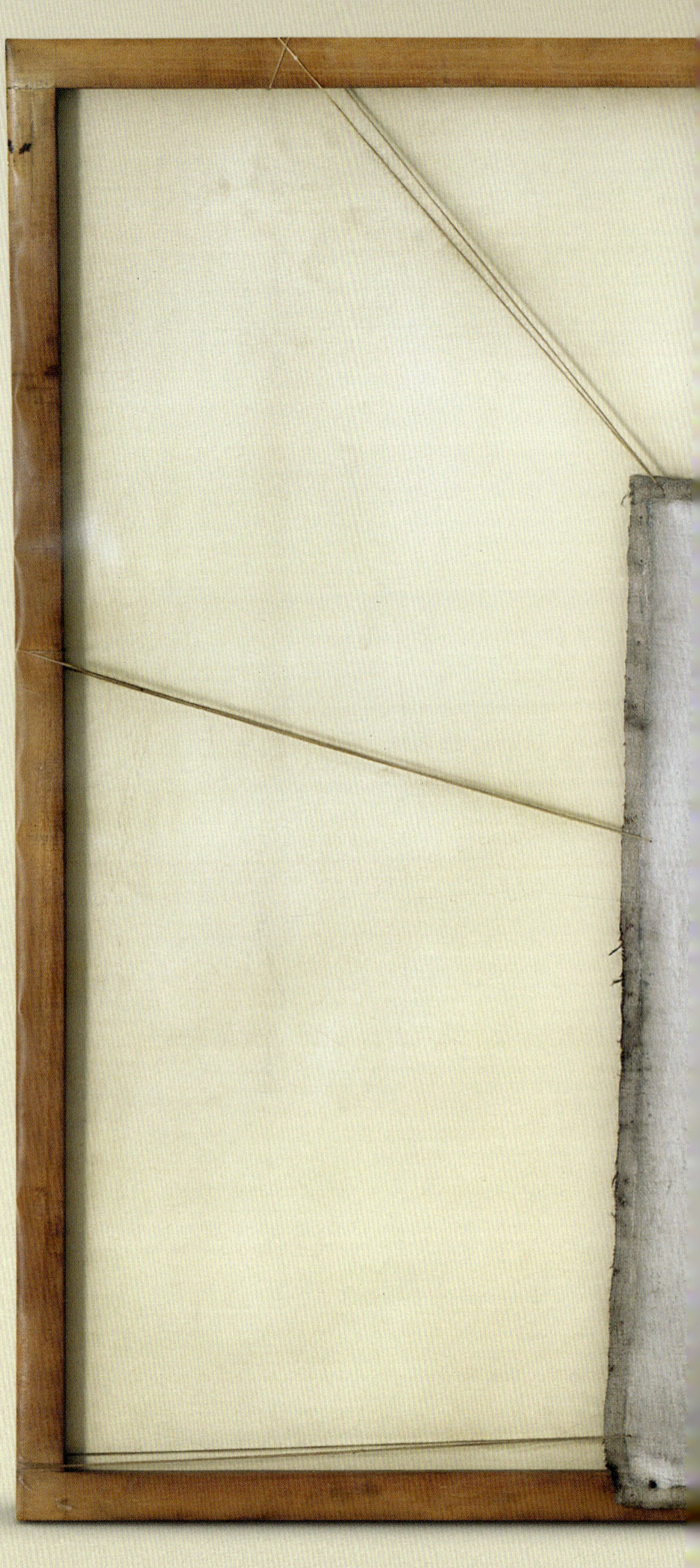

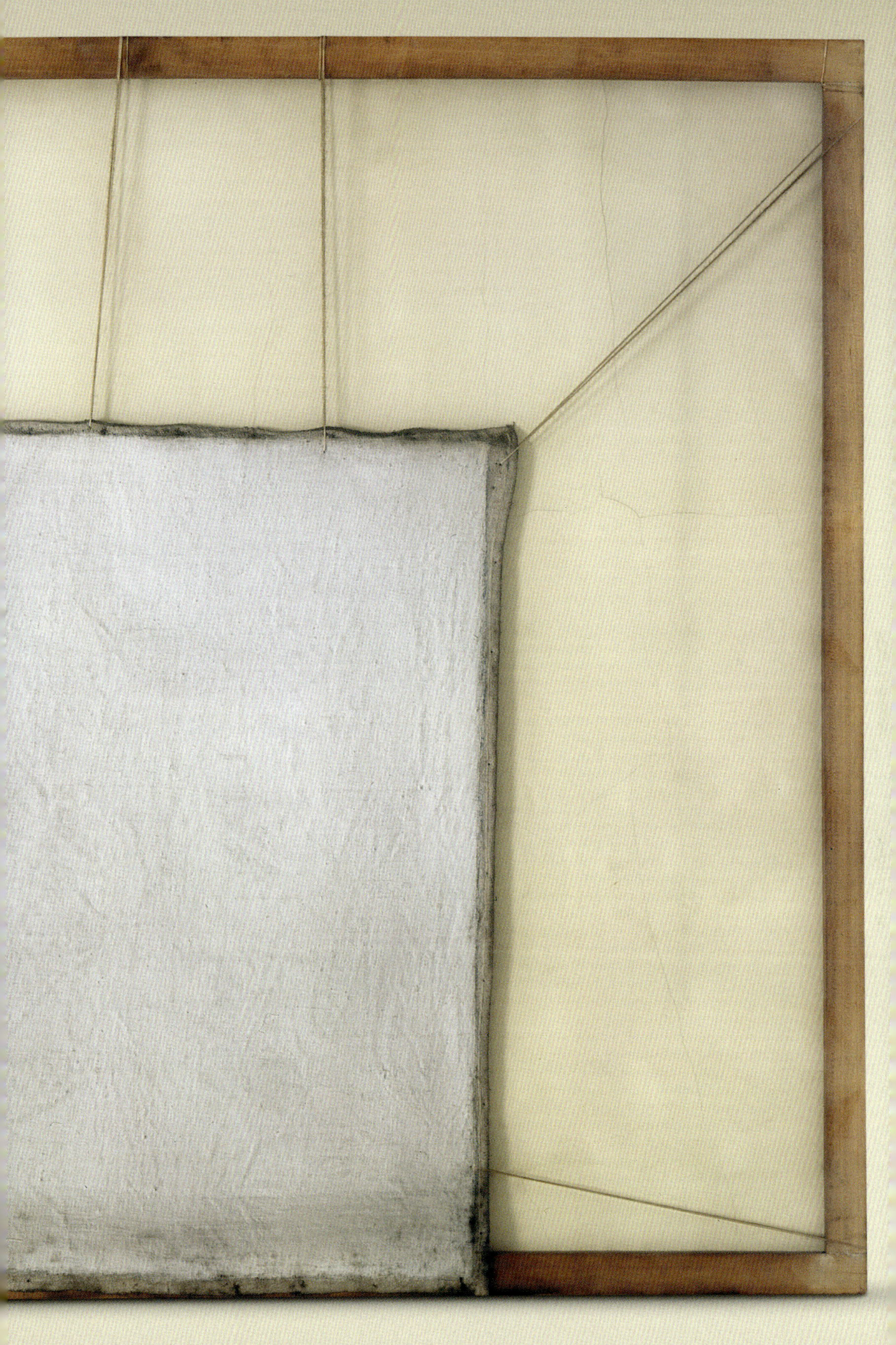

AN EMPTY WOODEN FRAME WHICH DEFINES SPACE
BY CONVENTION.
THE CANVAS IS REPLACED BY CLEAR PLASTIC,
BUT A SMALLER-SIZE FRAME HANGS BY SOME THREADS
IN THE FRAMED SPACE AS IF IT WERE THE "SUBJECT"
OF THE PAINTING.

GIULIO PAOLINI

In Germano Celant, *Giulio Paolini*, Sonnabend Press, New York 1972

GIULIO PAOLINI
Genoa 1940

Jasper Johns, 1967
paper, acrylic on
canvas
94 x 70 cm

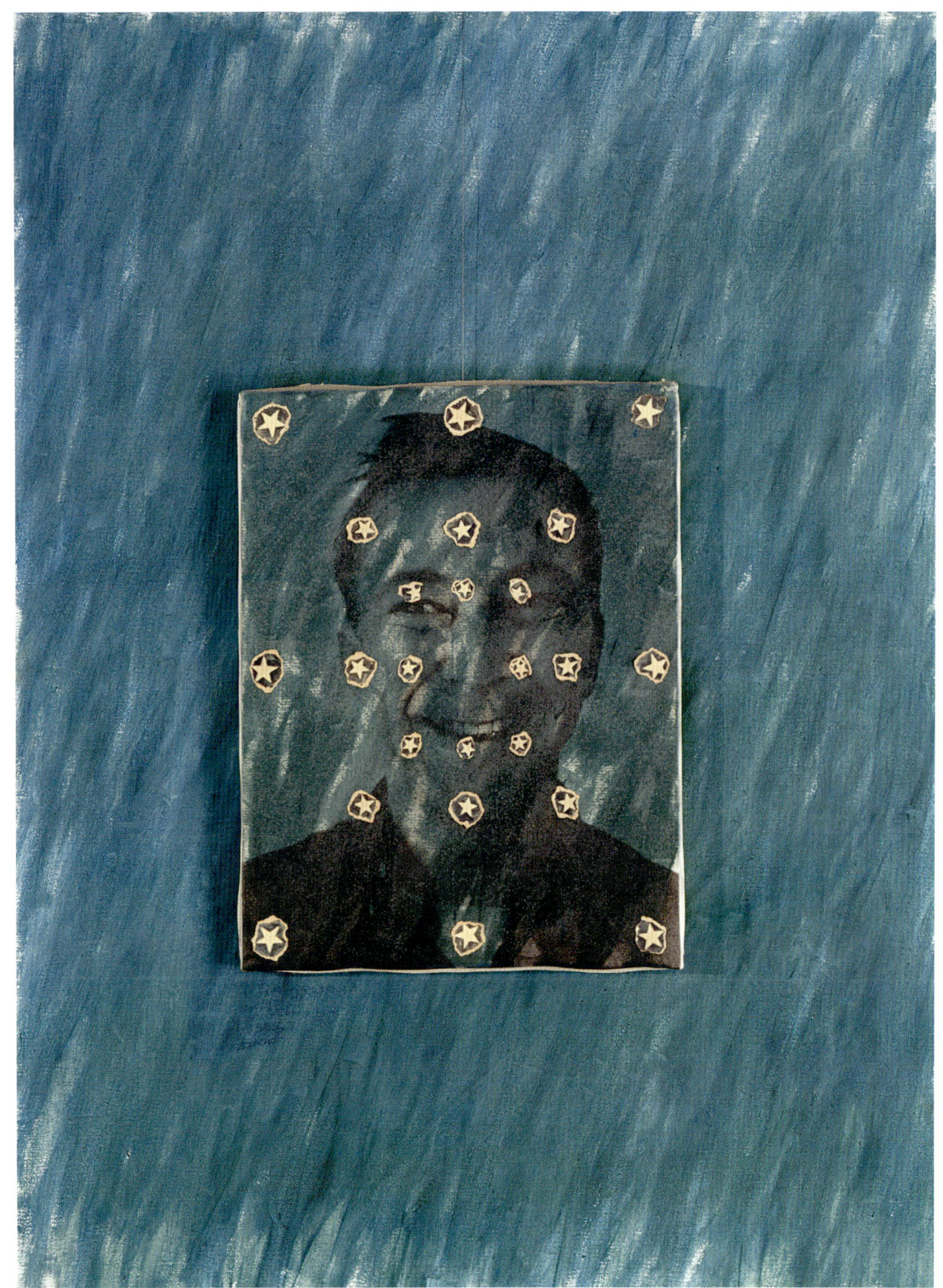

MATTER AND SPACE

YVES KLEIN
Nice 1928 - Paris 1962

IKB99, 1960
natural pigment,
synthetic resin,
canvas, masonite,
wooden stretcher
78 x 56 cm

ALBERTO BURRI
Città di Castello 1915 – Nice 1995

Bianco Rosso [White Red], 1954
burlap, fabric, oil, pumice, canvas, Vinavil glue on pressed cardboard
75 x 59 cm

WORDS AREN'T HELPFUL WHENEVER I TRY TO SPEAK OF MY PAINTING. AN UNYIELDING PRESENCE THAT REFUSES TO LET ITSELF BE TRANSFORMED INTO ANY OTHER FORM OF EXPRESSION.
A DIRECT, LIVELY PRESENCE. IN OTHER WORDS: EXISTING IS PAINTING. [...]
THE MOST I CAN SAY IS THAT, FOR ME, PAINTING IS FREEDOM ACHIEVED, CONSTANTLY STRENGTHENED, VIGILANTLY PRESERVED SO AS TO DRAW FROM IT THE STRENGTH TO KEEP ON PAINTING.

ALBERTO BURRI

In *The New Decade. 22 European Painters and Sculptors*, exhibition catalogue (New York, The Museum of Modern Art, 1955), Connecticut Printers, Hartford 1955

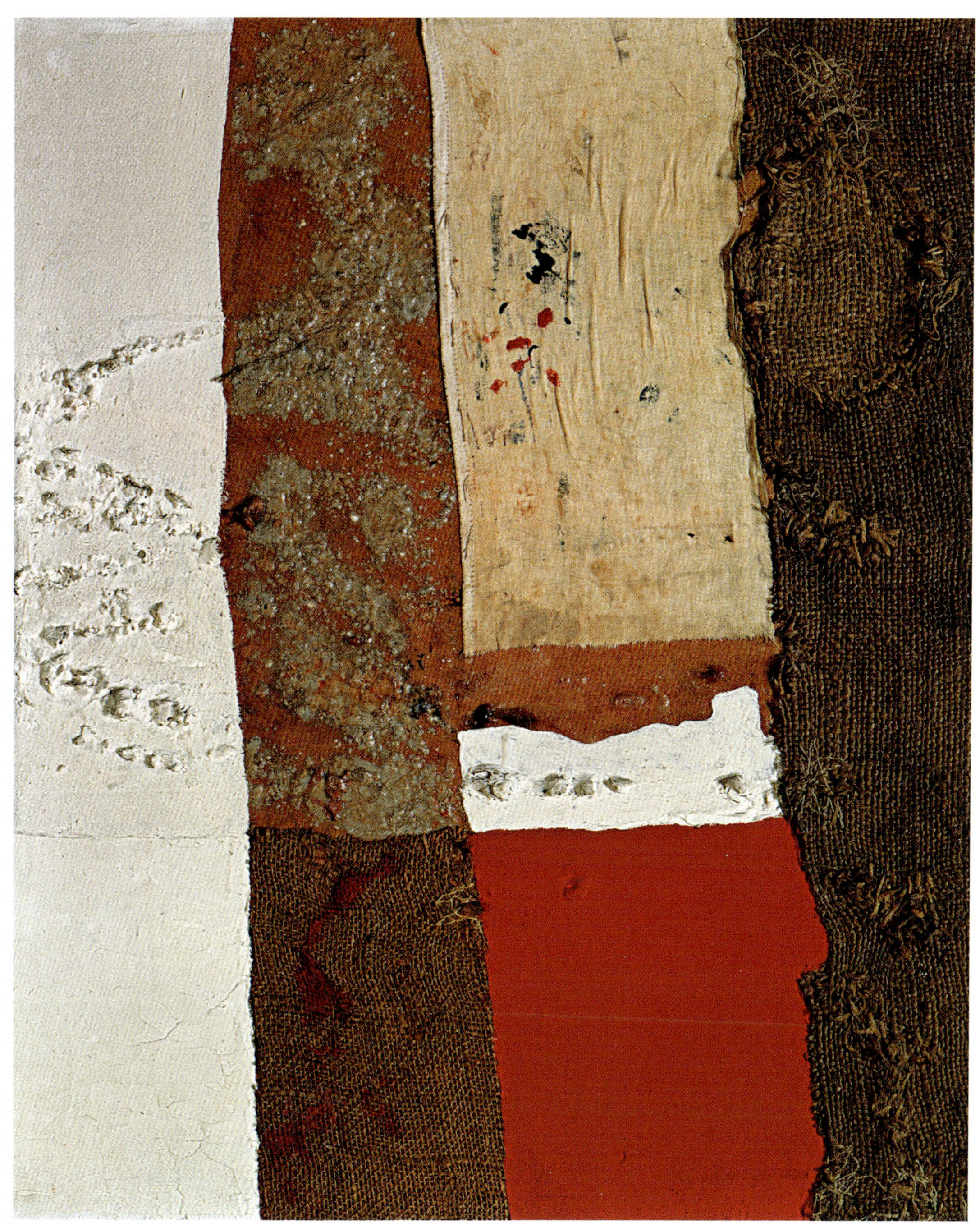

LUCIO FONTANA
Rosario, Santa Fe 1899 –
Comabbio 1968

Concetto spaziale [Spatial Concept], 1957
aniline dye and collage on perforated canvas
250 x 200 cm

on the following pages

LUCIO FONTANA
Rosario, Santa Fe 1899 –
Comabbio 1968

Concetto spaziale. Attese [Spatial Concept. Expectations], 1965
water paint on canvas
130 x 195 cm

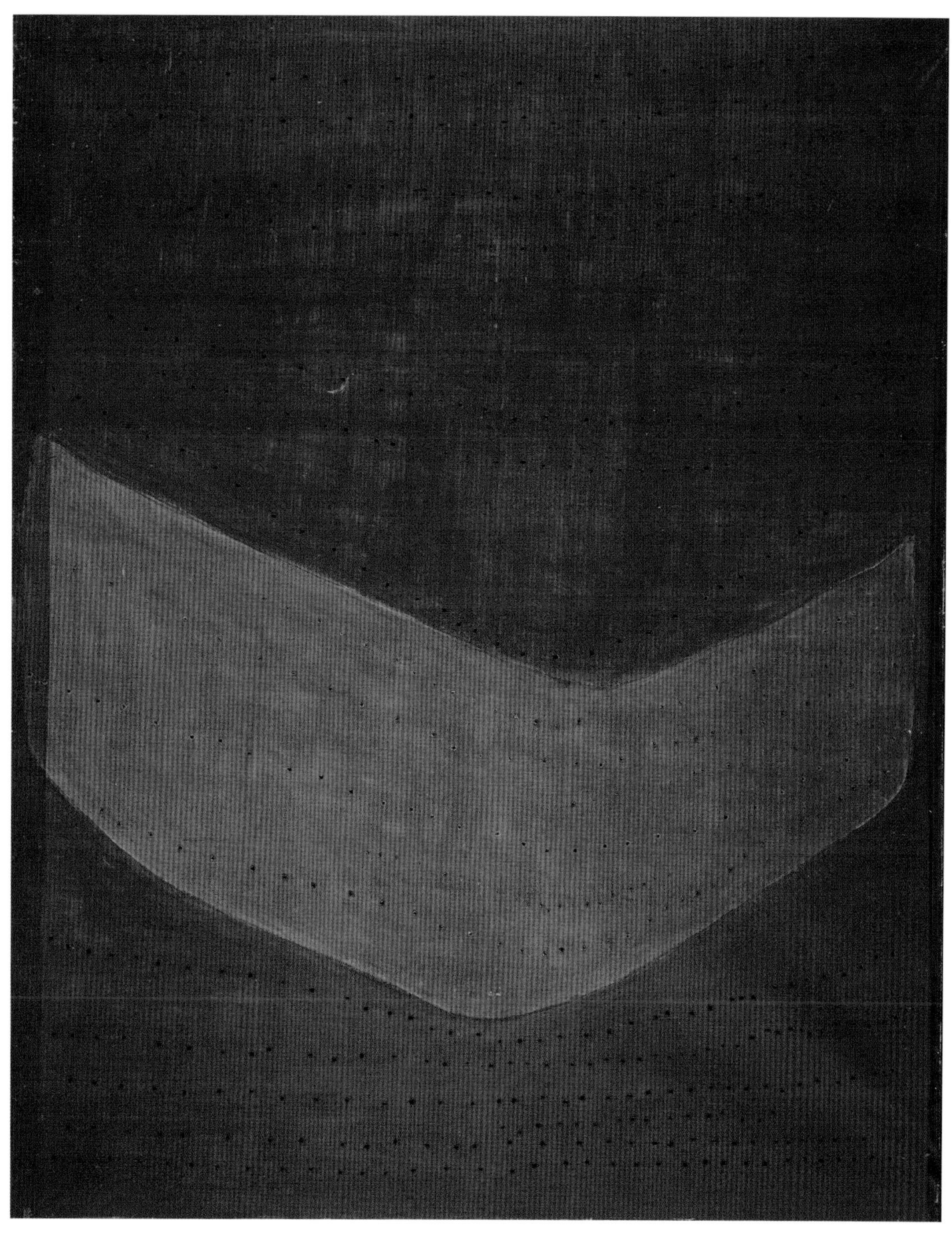

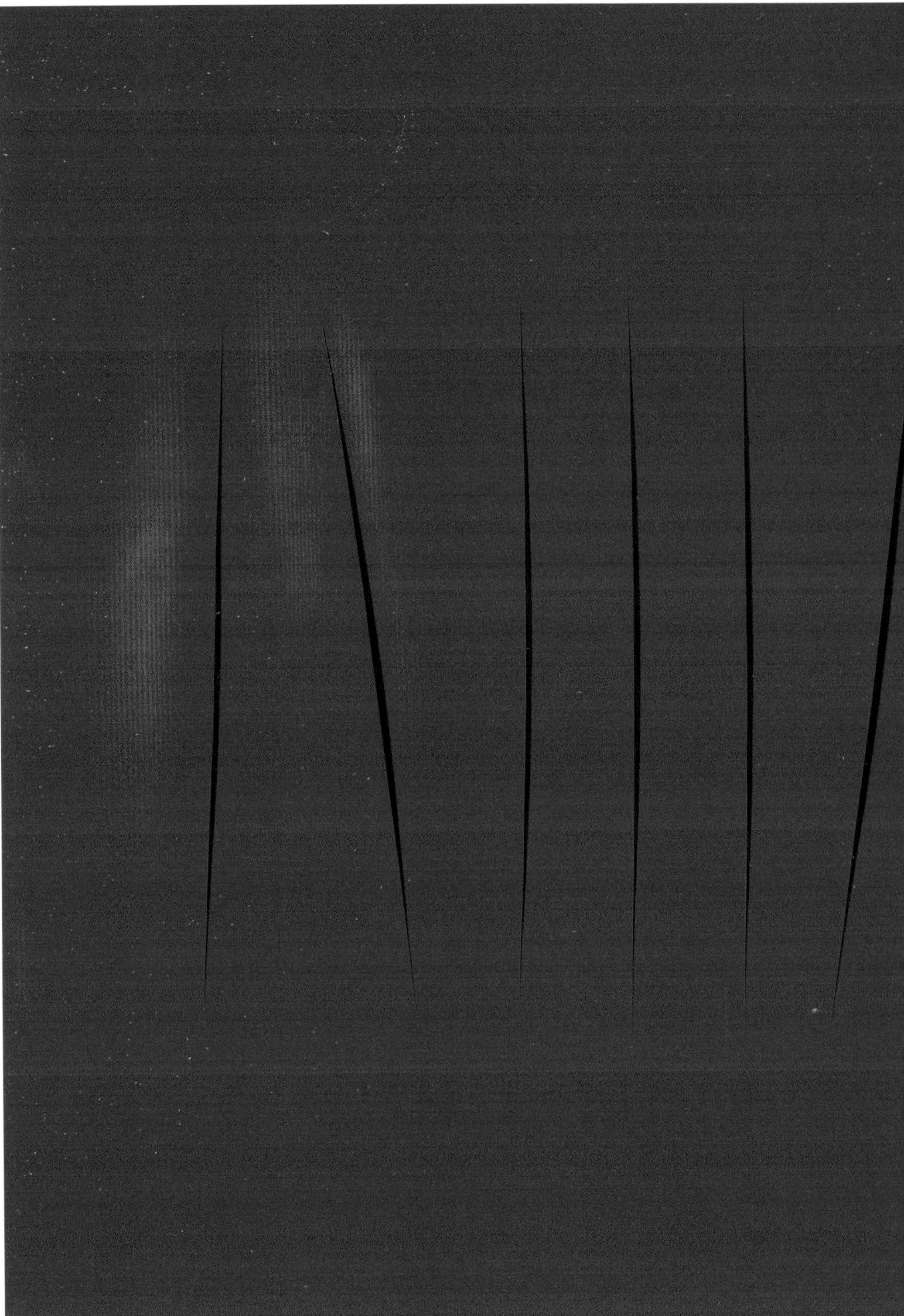

LUCIO FONTANA
Rosario, Santa Fe 1899 –
Comabbio 1968

Concetto spaziale. Teatrino [Spatial Concept. Little Theatre], 1965
water paint on canvas, lacquered wood
130 x 130 cm

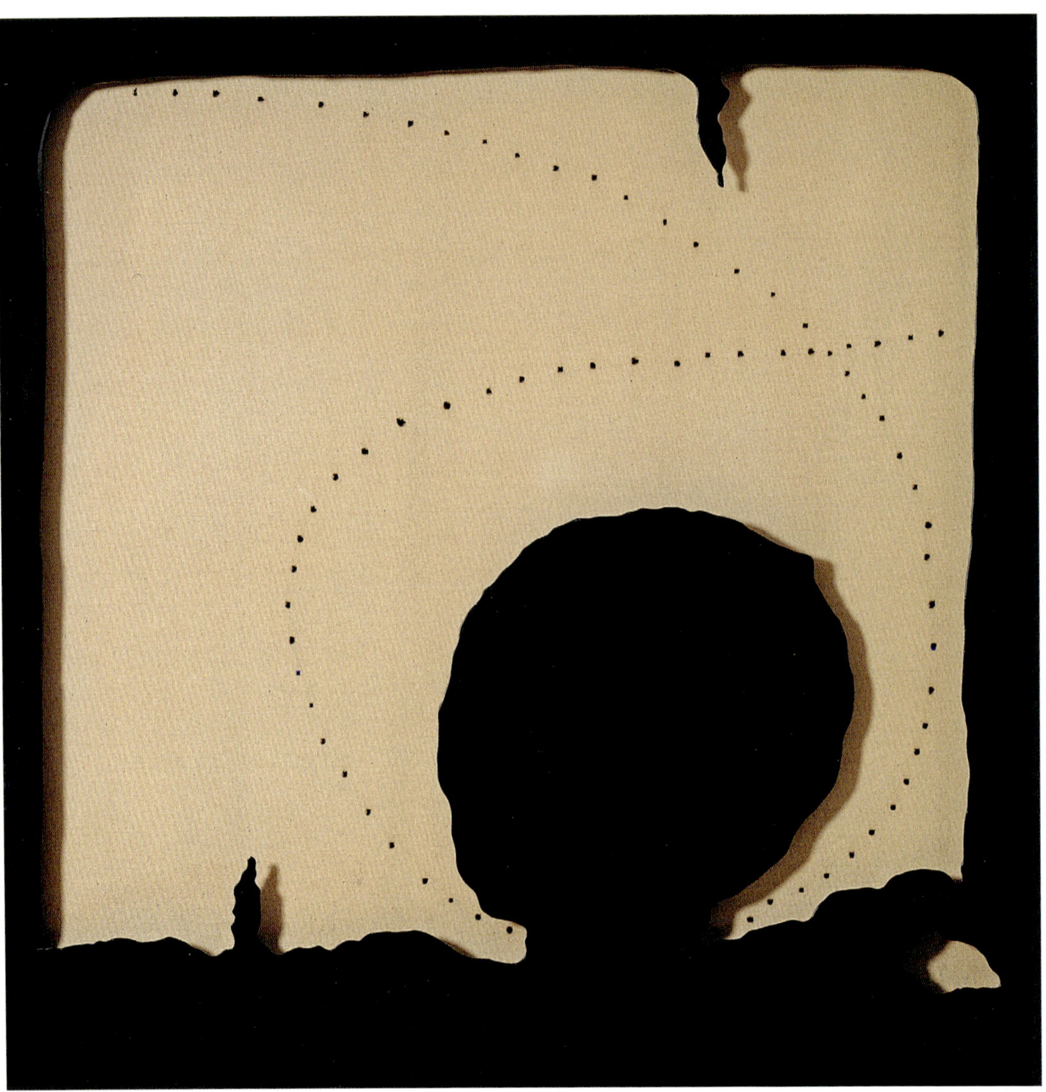

EVEN THE WORKS I WAS MAKING IN 1946 I NEVER CALLED PAINTINGS. I ALWAYS REFERRED TO THEM AS 'SPATIAL CONCEPTS.' THIS IS BECAUSE, FOR ME, PAINTING RESIDES ENTIRELY IN THE IDEA. THE CANVAS IS WHAT I NEEDED, AND STILL NEED, TO DOCUMENT AN IDEA. THE WORKS I AM MAKING NOW ARE JUST VARIATIONS ON MY TWO KEY CONCEPTS: THE HOLE AND THE CUT. AT A TIME WHEN PEOPLE WERE TALKING ABOUT 'PLANES' – THE SURFACE PLANE, THE DEPTH PLANE ETC. –, TO MAKE A HOLE WAS A RADICAL GESTURE THAT BROKE THE SPACE OF THE CANVAS AS IF TO SAY: AFTER THIS WE ARE FREE TO DO WHATEVER WE LIKE.

LUCIO FONTANA

Interview with Lucio Fontana by Daniela Palazzoli, in "bit", no. 5, Milan, October-November 1967

LUCIO FONTANA
Rosario, Santa Fe 1899 –
Comabbio 1968

Concetto spaziale. Natura [Spatial Concept. Nature], (1960) 1982
bronze
57 x 65 cm

Concetto spaziale. Natura [Spatial Concept. Nature], (1960) 1982
bronze
57 x 65 cm

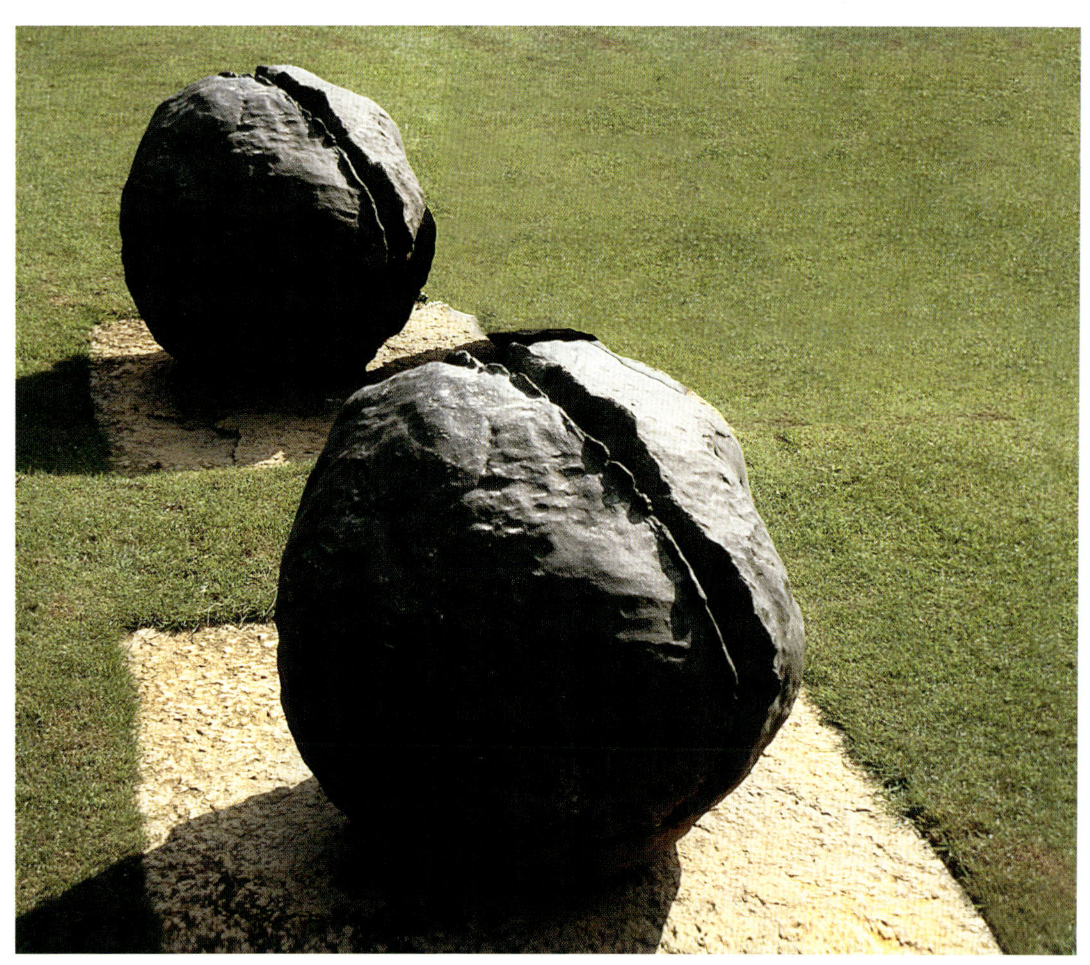

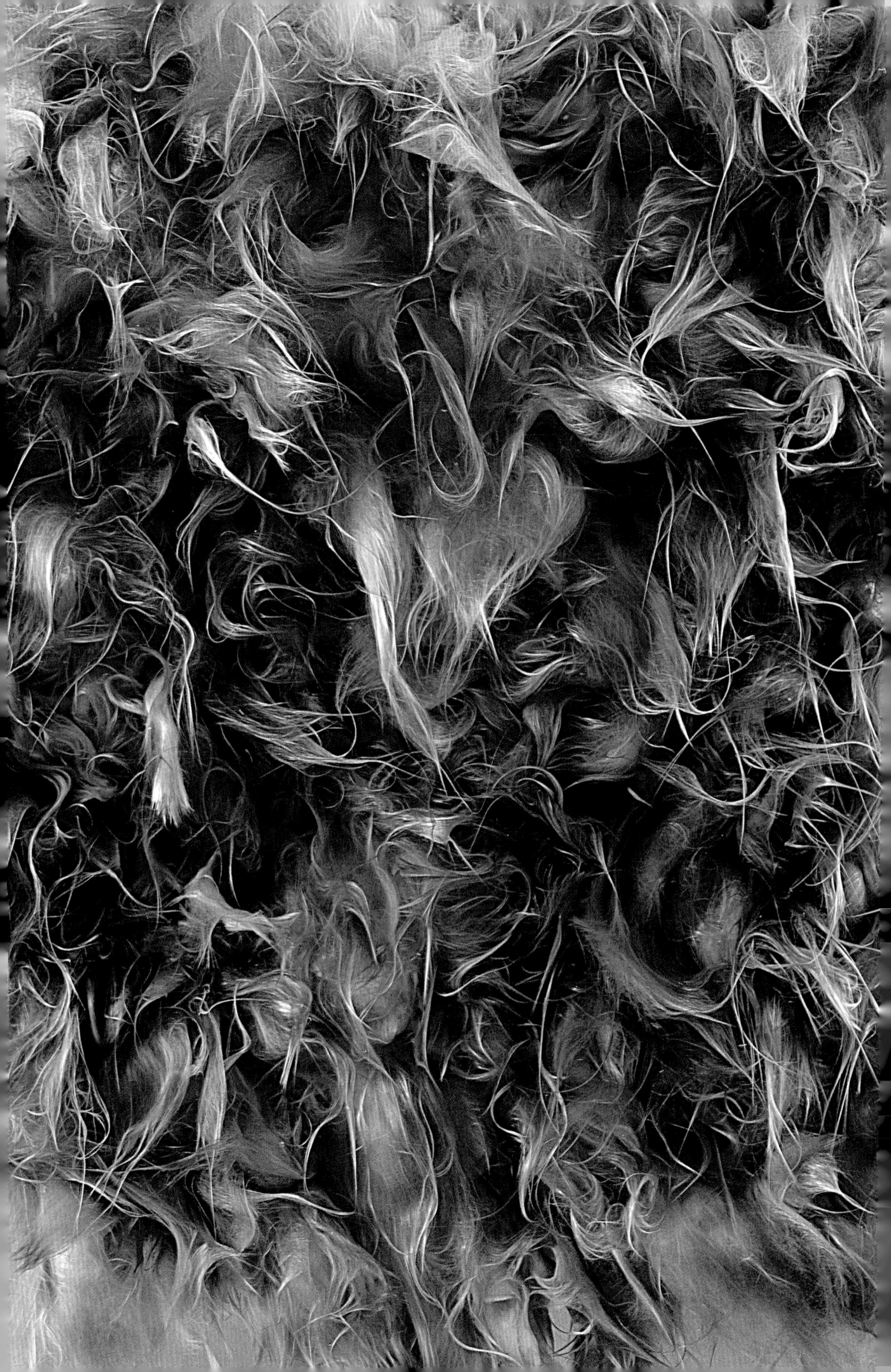

FROM MONOCHROME ZEROING TO THE IDEA OF CONCEPTUAL ART

AS NEW CONDITIONS ARISE AND NEW PROBLEMS SURFACE, WE FEEL THE NEED FOR NEW SOLUTIONS, NEW METHODS AND MEAURES; WE CAN NO LONGER BREAK AWAY FROM THE GROUND BY RUNNING OR JUMPING: WE NEED WINGS NOW, CHANGES ARE NO LONGER ENOUGH; OUR TRANSFORMATION MUST BE COMPLETE. THIS IS WHY I AM UNABLE TO UNDERSTAND THE PAINTERS WHO – THOUGH CLAIMING TO BE INTERESTED IN MODERN ISSUES – STILL STAND BEFORE A CANVAS AS IF IT WERE A SURFACE TO BE FILLED WITH SHAPES AND COLOURS [...].
WHY NOT EMPTY THIS CONTAINER, EH? WHY NOT FREE THIS SURFACE? WHY NOT TRY AND DISCOVER THE BOUNDLESS MEANING OF A TOTAL SPACE, A PURE AND ABSOLUTE LIGHT?

PIERO MANZONI
Libera dimensione, in "Azimuth", no. 2, Milan, 1960

PIERO MANZONI
Soncino 1933 – Milan 1963

Achrome, 1961
artificial fibre
(glass wool)
100 x 80 x 20 cm

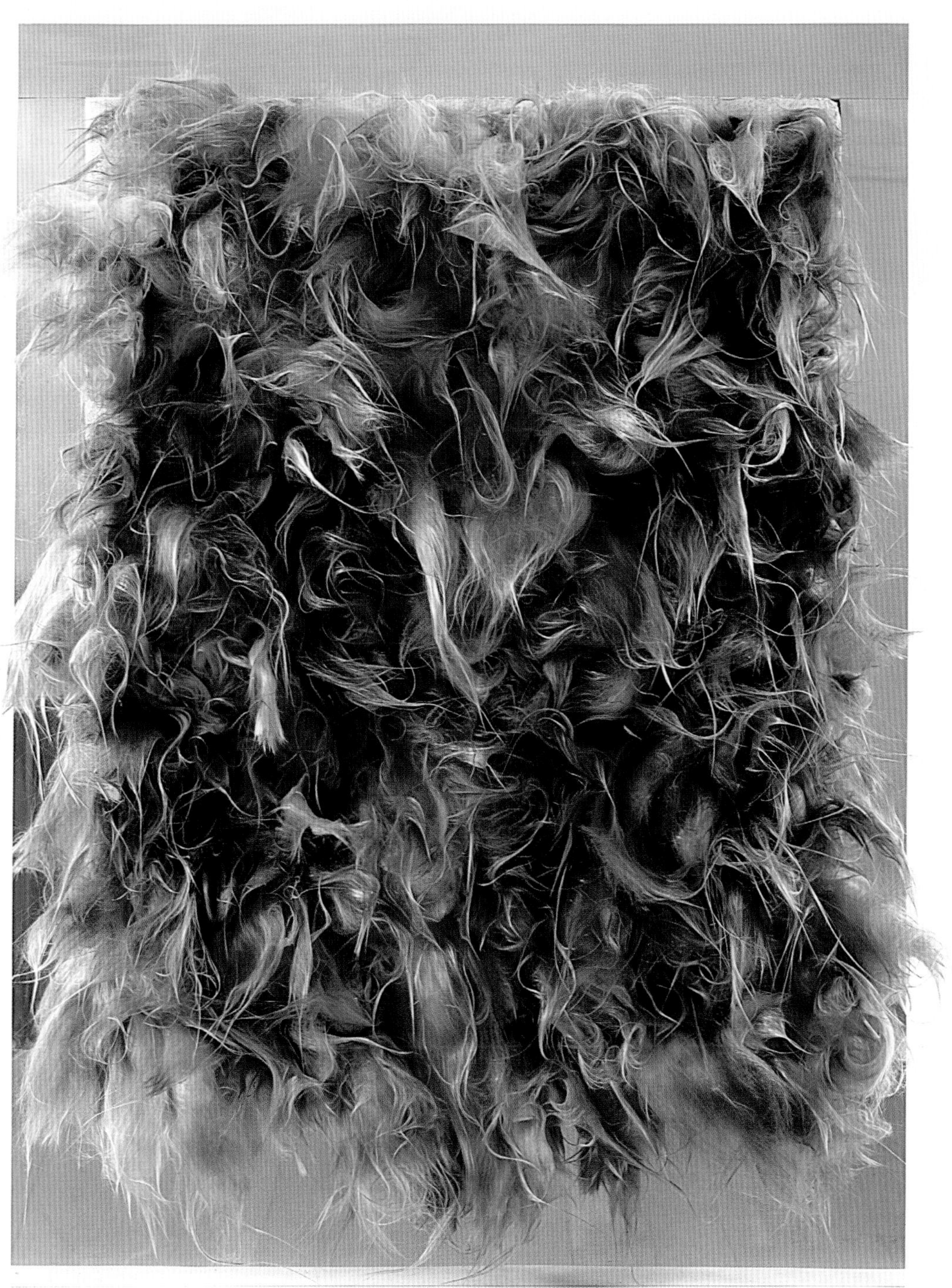

ENRICO
CASTELLANI
Castelmassa 1930 – Celleno
2017

Superficie Bianca. Dittico [White Surface. Diptych], 1967
tempera on convex, concave, and shaped canvas
120 x 150 cm

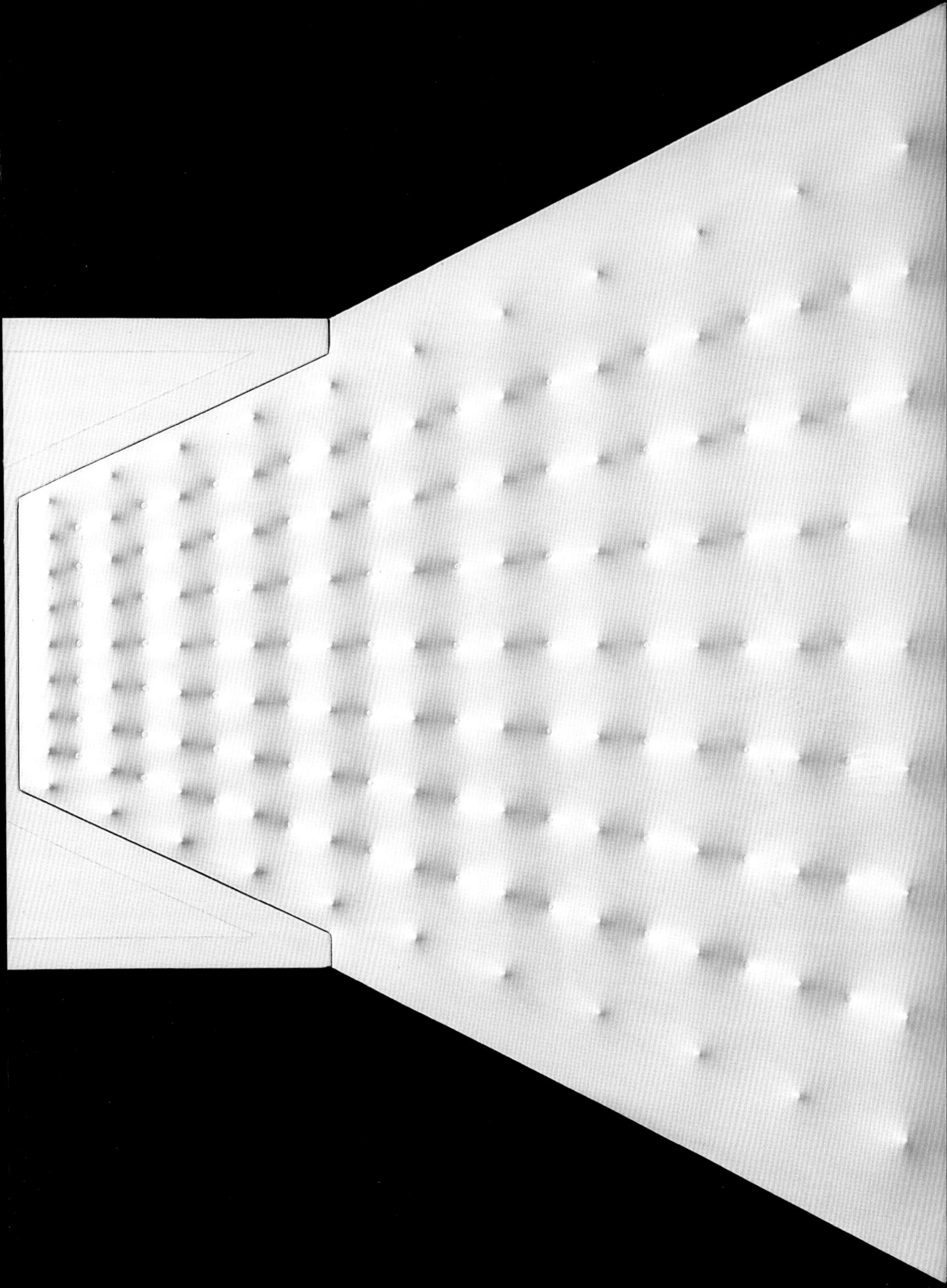

ROBERT RYMAN
Nashville, Tennessee 1930

Winsor 20, 1966
Winsor oil paint
on canvas
194,5 x 194,5 cm

THE SKY ACCOMPANIES ALL "TAUTOLOGIES"; I EXECUTED THE OTHERS AS I WAS CREATING IT (SIX MONTHS). I COPY THE MAP OF THE SKY, I BAR MY IMAGINATION WITH THE MANUAL ACTIVITY THAT IS TRANSCRIPTION. BUT THEN, DURING THE LONG LAPSE OF TIME TAKEN UP BY THIS TRANSCRIPTION, A VOID OPENS, AND FEELINGS START WELLING UP WITHIN.

LUCIANO FABRO

Il Cielo, in *Luciano Fabro. Letture parallele IV*, exhibition catalogue (Milan, PAC, Padiglione d'arte Contemporanea, April-May 1980), Silvana Editoriale, Cinisello Balsamo 1980

LUCIANO FABRO
Turin 1936 – Milan 2007

Avanti dietro destra sinistra. Tautologia (Cielo) [Front Back Right Left. Tautology (Sky)], 1967-1968
painted iron, enamel paint
250 x 356 cm
(three panels)

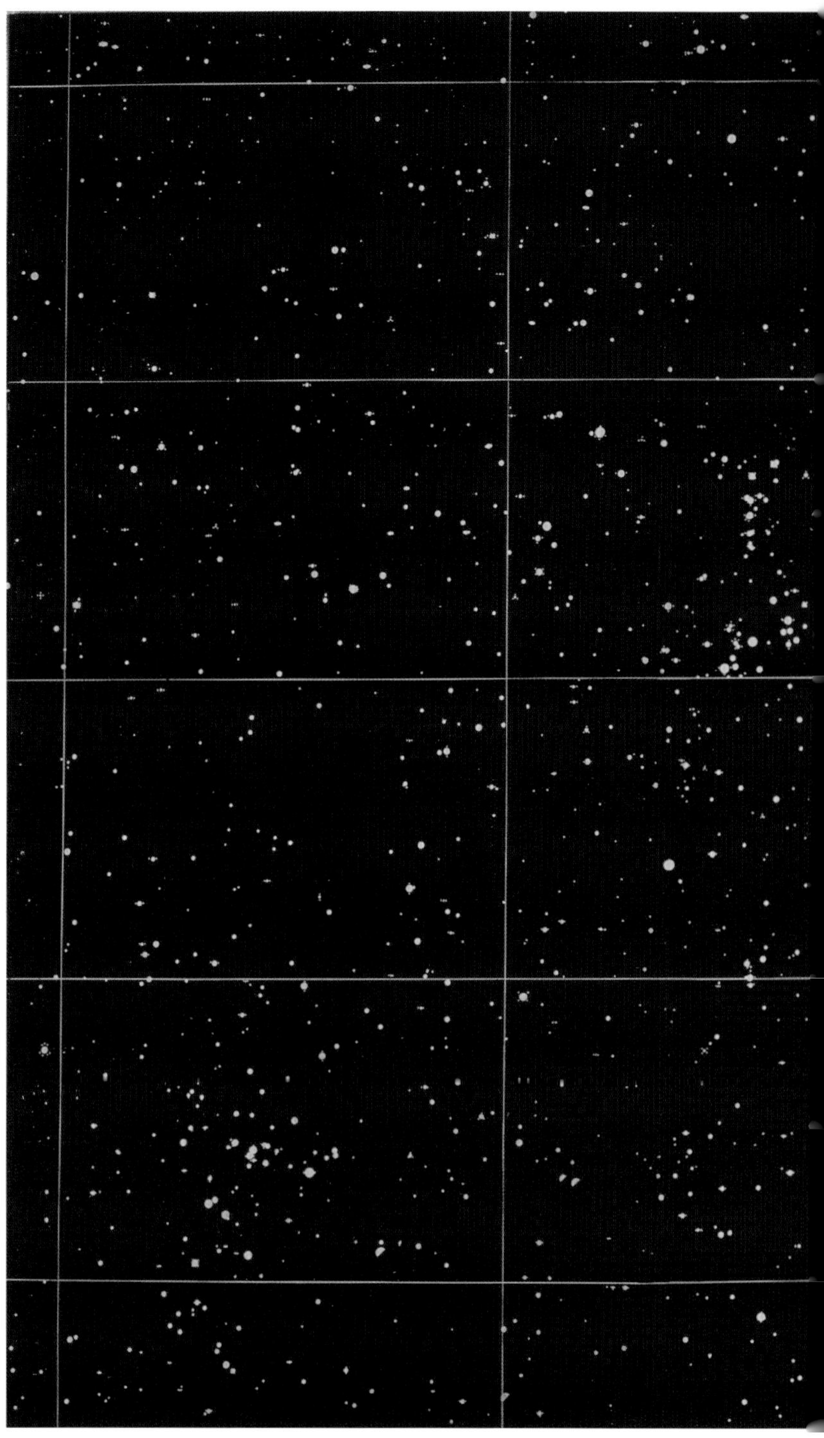

I BELIEVE THAT EVERYTHING CONTAINS ITS OPPOSITE, THEREFORE THE BEST ATTITUDE IS THE ZEROING OF CONCEPTS – UNFOLDING AND SPREADING THEM OUT LIKE A SHEET OF PAPER. THUS WE CAN ARRANGE AND DISARRANGE A PAIR OR CATEGORY OF CONCEPTS, NEVER FAVOURING ONE OF THE TWO OPPOSITES BUT, RATHER, ALWAYS SEARCHING FOR ONE WITHIN THE OTHER. ORDER WITHIN DISORDER, THE NATURAL WITHIN THE ARTIFICIAL, SHADOW WITHIN LIGHT... AND VICE VERSA.

ALIGHIERO BOETTI

Dall'oggi al domani, edited by S. Lombardi, Edizioni L'Obliquo, Brescia 1988

ALIGHIERO
BOETTI
Turin 1940 – Rome 1994

Ononimo, 1973
red ball pen on
carboard
11 elements
70 x 100 cm each

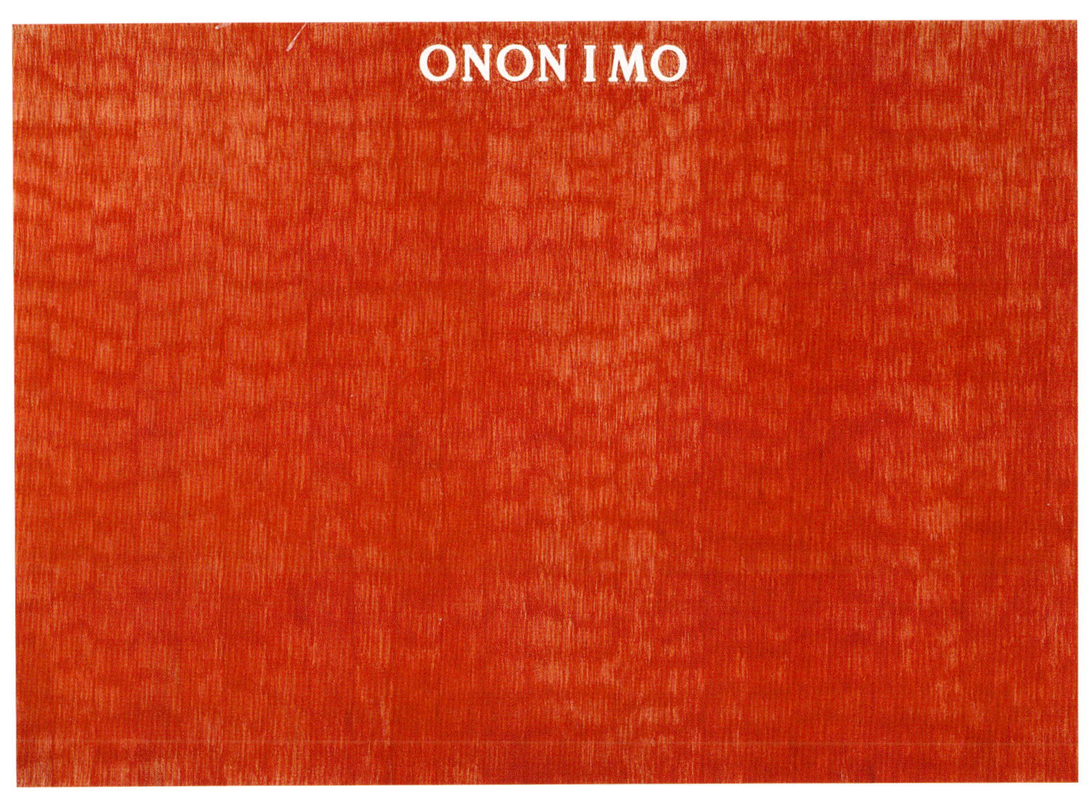

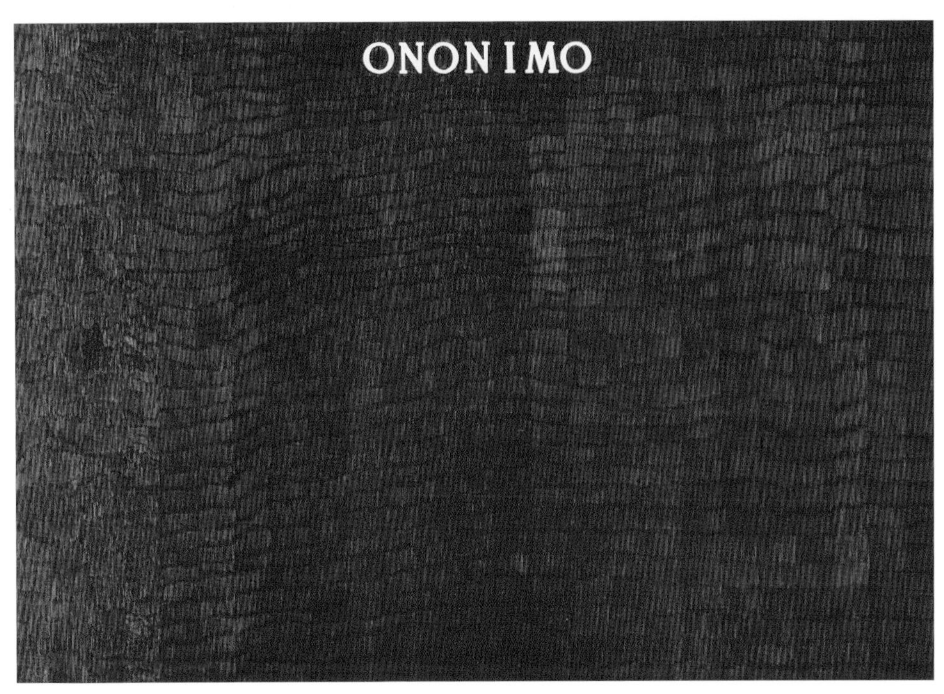
ONONIMO

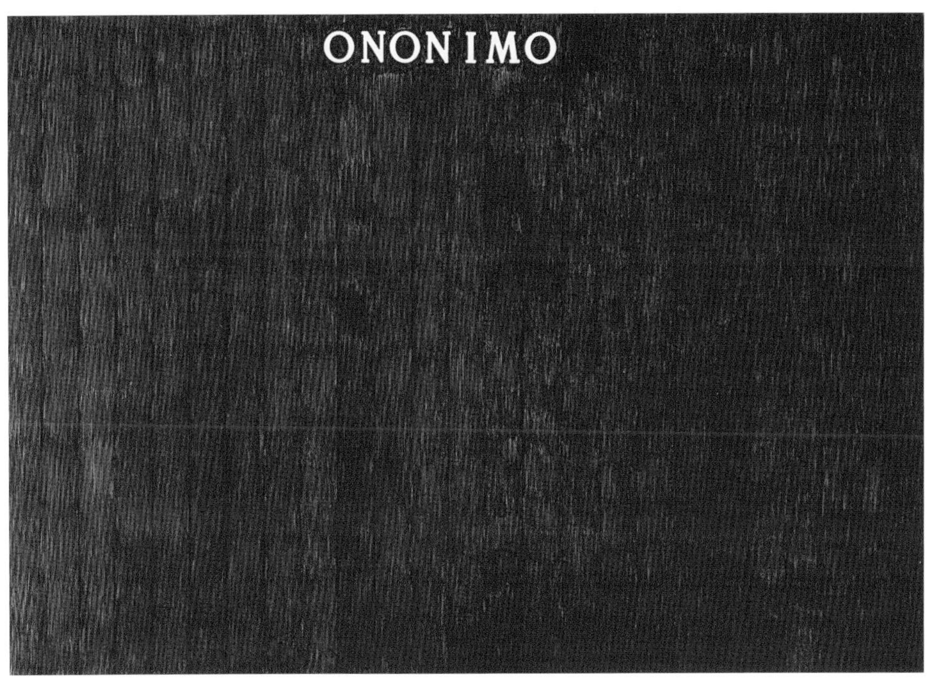
ONONIMO

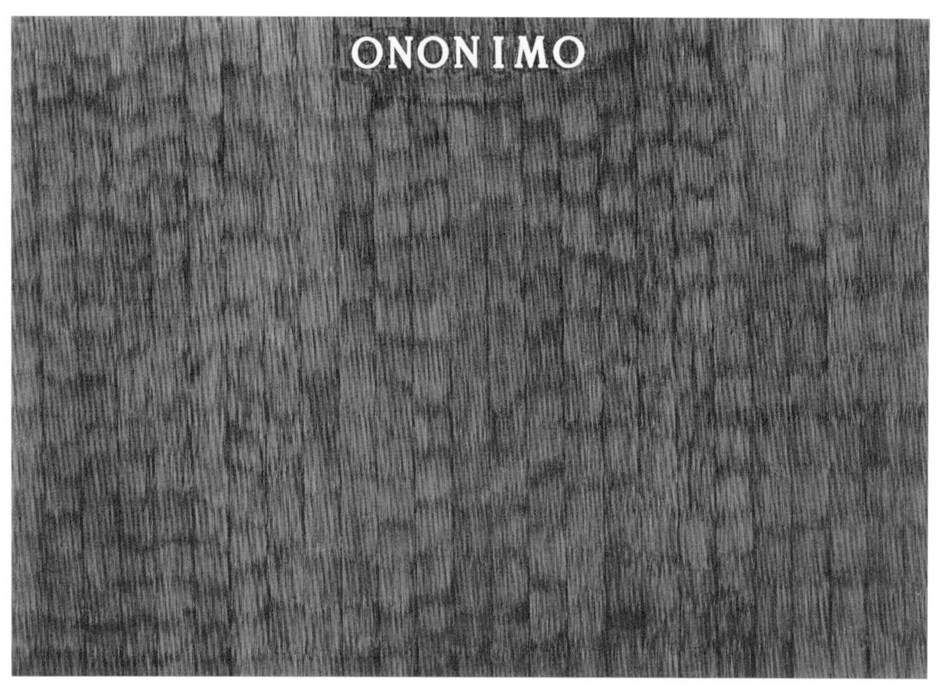
ONONIMO

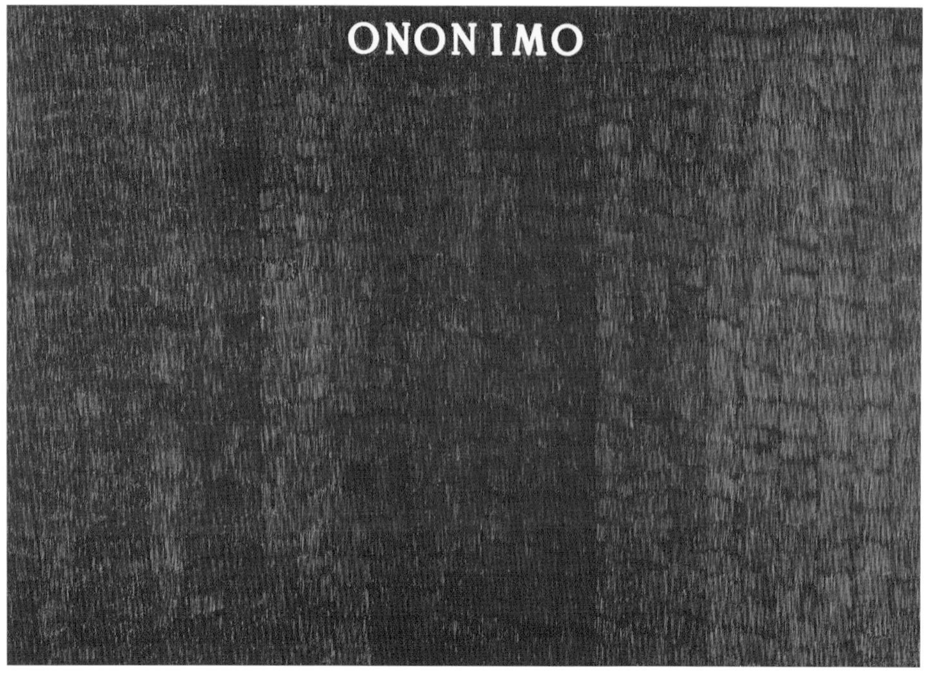
ONONIMO

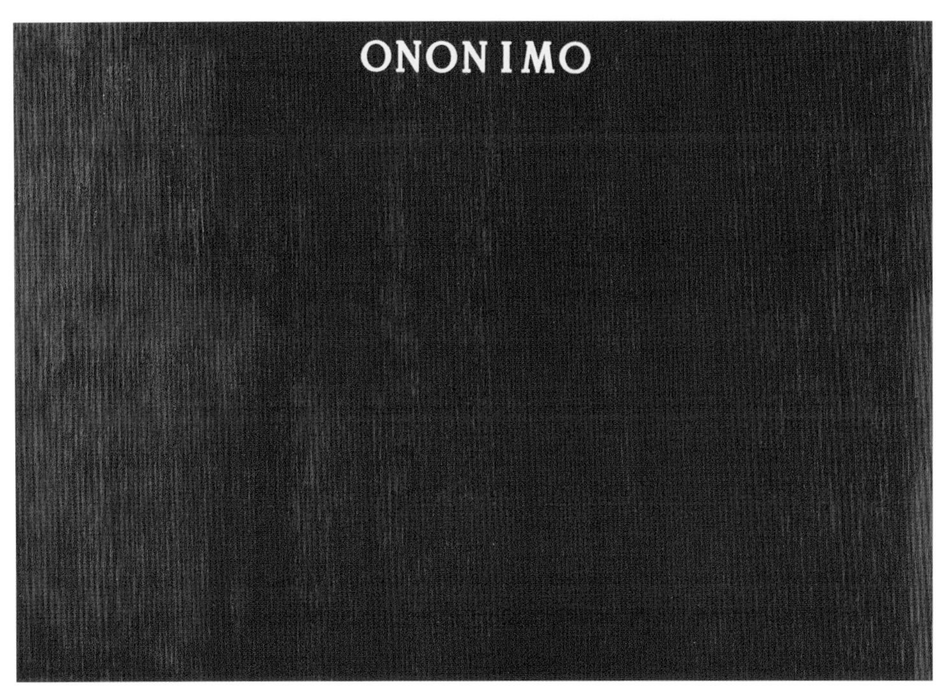
ONONIMO

ONONIMO

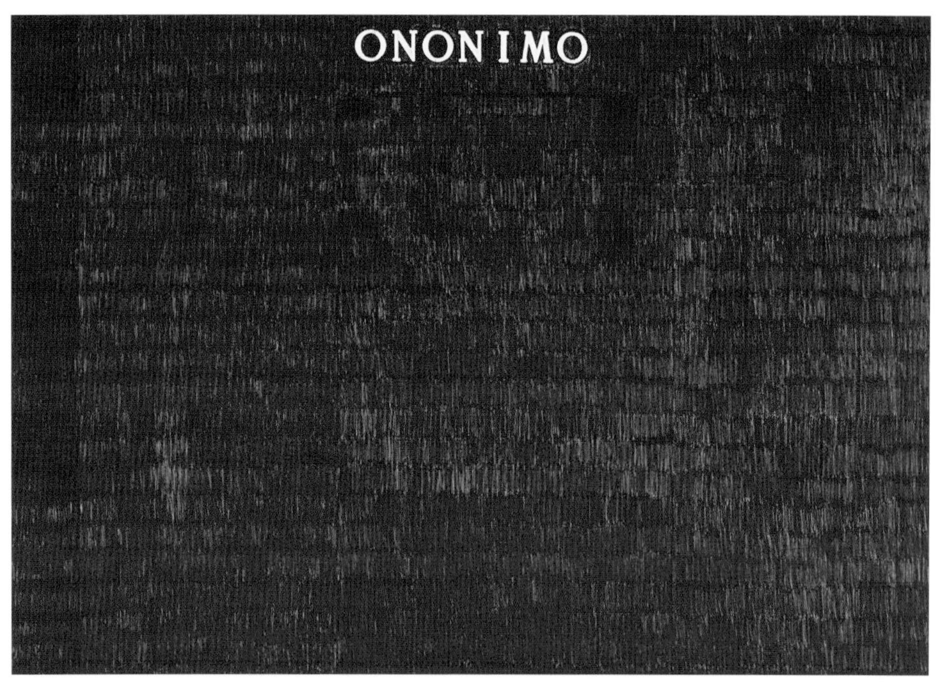
ONONIMO

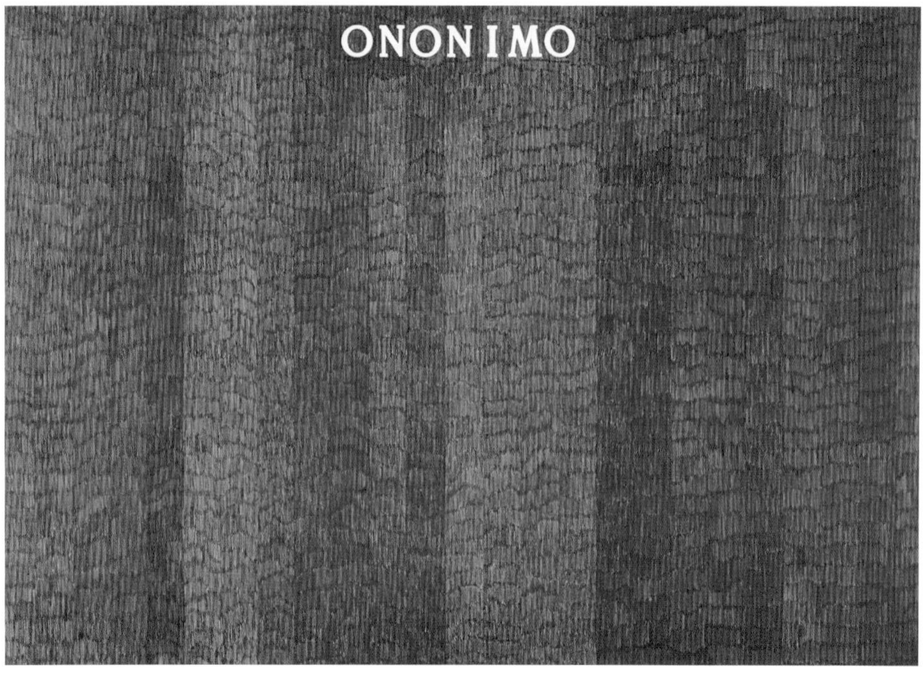
ONONIMO

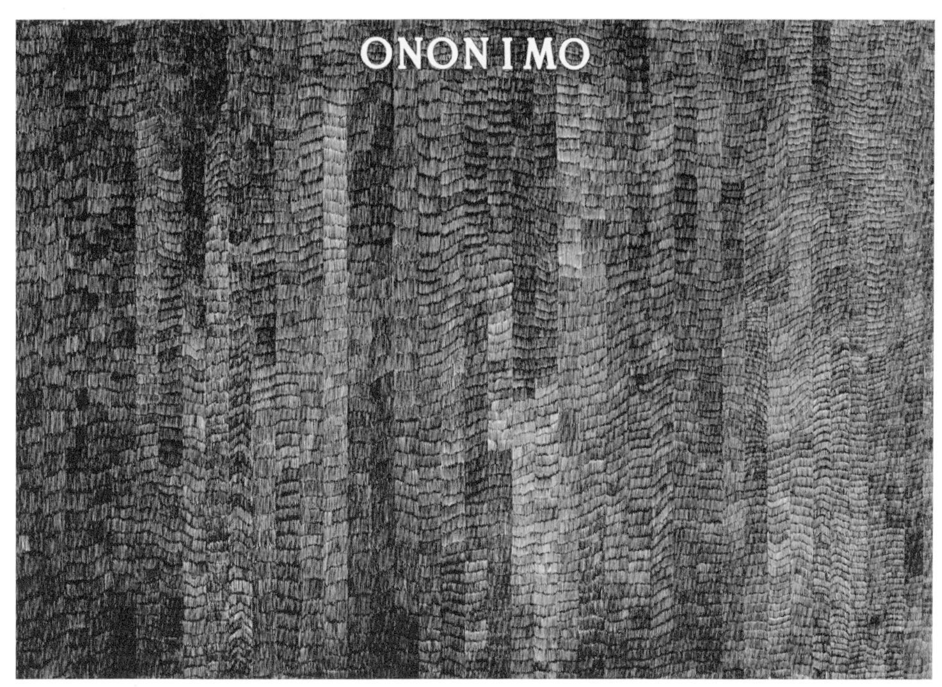
ONONIMO

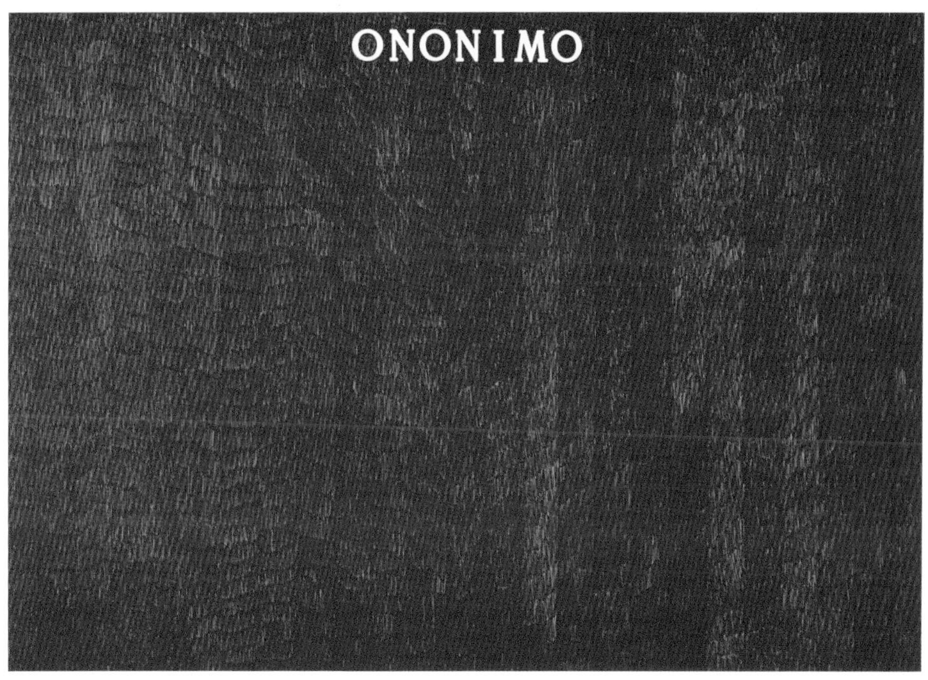
ONONIMO

AN AUTHOR PURCHASED BY THE AGRATI BROTHERS BY VIRTUE OF HIS INTELLECTUAL SOPHISTICATION, FROM THE LATE FIFTIES ONWARDS AGNETTI PROVED HIMSELF ONE OF THE KEENEST THINKERS TO THEORISE A NEW ART WITHIN THE LIVELY MILANESE CULTURAL CONTEXT. IN THESE WORKS, THE ARTIST ENGRAVED WORDS OR BRIEF SENTENCES ON FELT AND BAKELITE SHEETS, ENHANCING THE WORDS THEMSELVES AND THEIR OBJECTIVITY TO THE UTMOST. HIS BODY OF WORK, WHICH FEATURES A MARKED CONCEPTUAL CONNOTATION, IS COMPARABLE TO THAT OF OTHER AUTHORS WHO INVESTIGATED LANGUAGE, SUCH AS AMERICAN ARTIST JOSEPH KOSUTH, REPRESENTED IN THE COLLECTION BY TITLED (ART AS IDEA AS IDEA). AIR. ALONG WITH THE OTHER COLLECTIONS IN THIS SECTION, THESE WORKS ATTEST TO THE AGRATI BROTHERS' INTEREST IN THE MORE CONCEPTUAL, MINIMAL SIDE OF ARTISTIC RESEARCH.

VINCENZO AGNETTI
Milan 1926-1981

In questo luogo si possono contare le ore e le dita [In This Place You Can Count the Hours and the Fingers], 1970
gold nitrocellulose paint, pyrographed felt applied on panel
80 x 118 cm

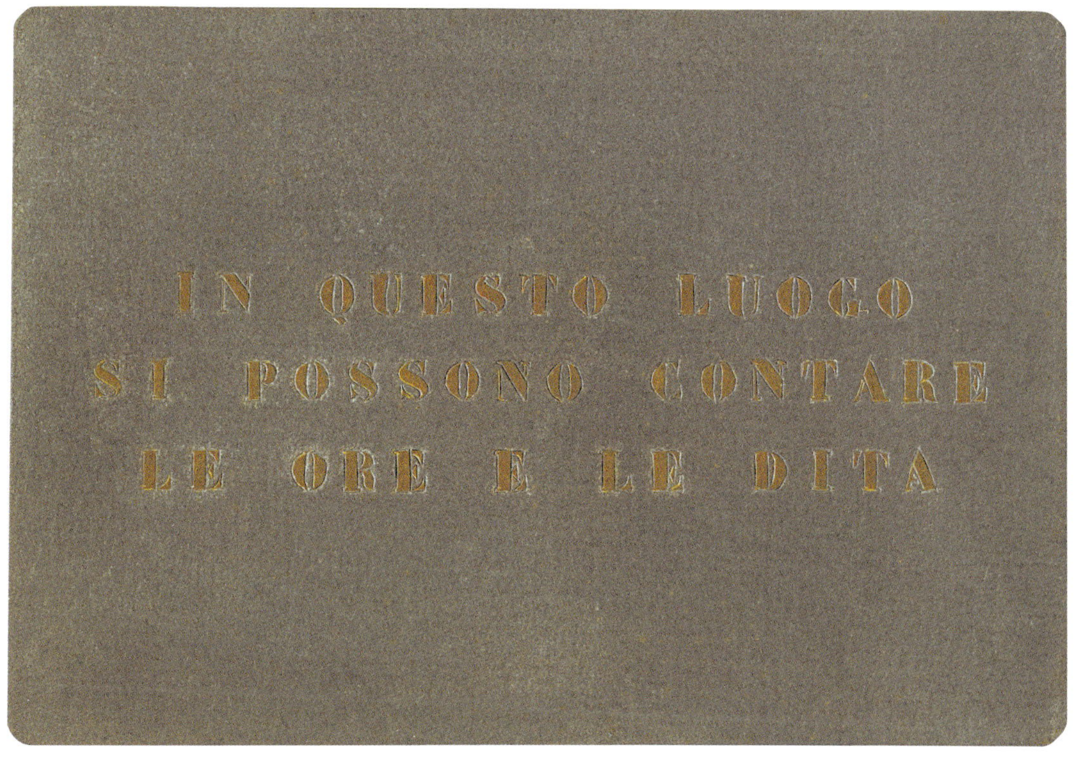

VINCENZO AGNETTI
Milan 1926-1981

Assioma. Cultura quasi dimenticata a memoria Culture Almost Forgotten by Heart [Axiom. Cultura quasi dimenticata a memoria Culture Almost Forgotten by Heart], 1972
engraved Bakelite sheet
80 x 80 cm

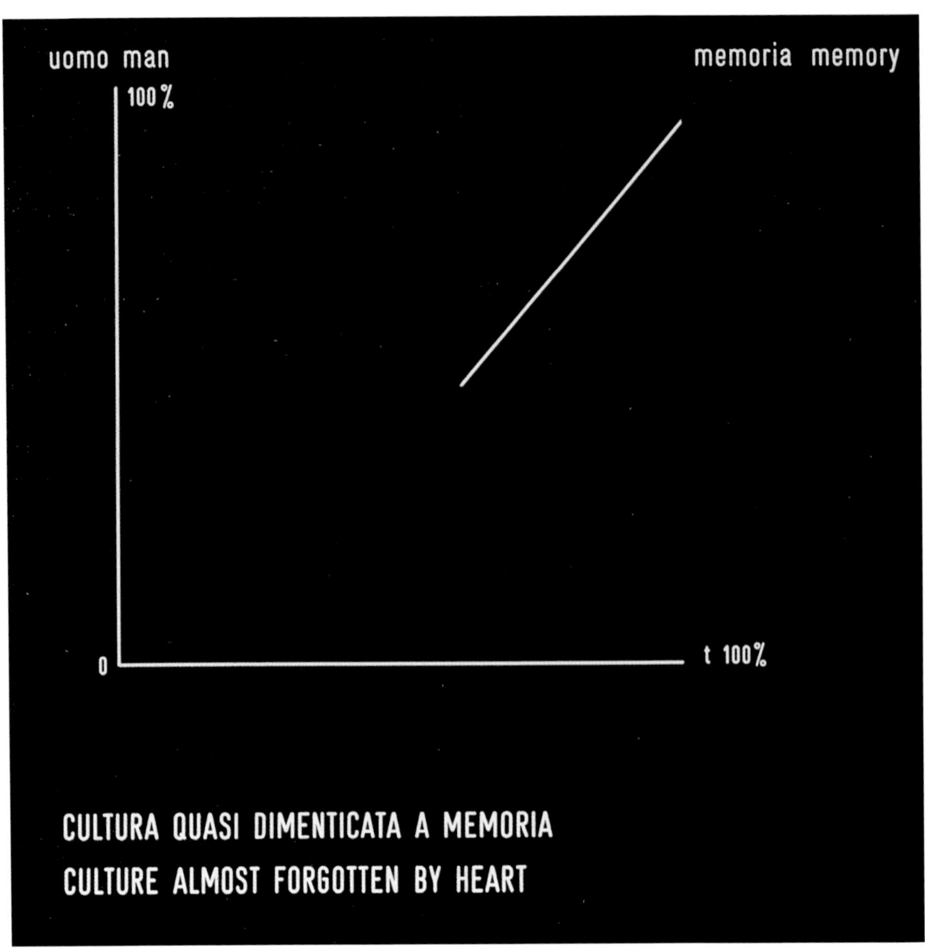

VINCENZO AGNETTI
Milan 1926 -1981

Assioma. Territorio Territory [Axiom. Territorio Territory], 1972
engraved Bakelite sheet
80 x 80 cm

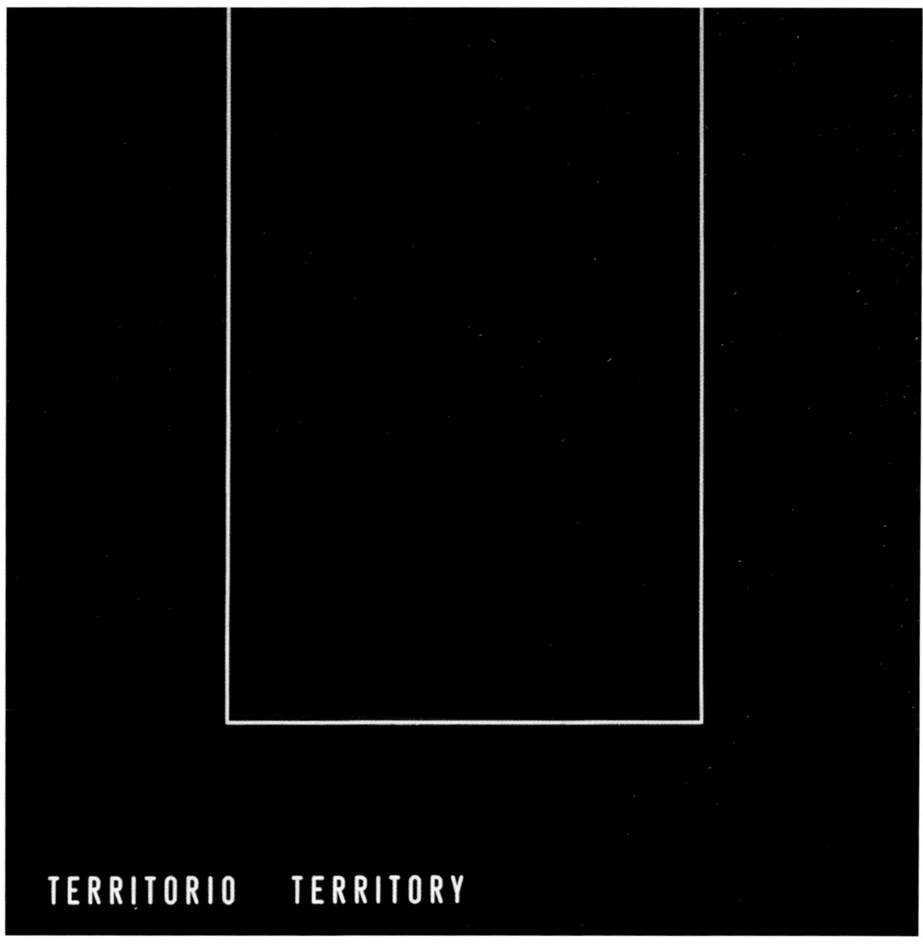

JOSEPH KOSUTH
Toledo, Ohio 1945

Titled (Art as Idea as Idea). Air, 1966-1968
photographic enlargment on paper mounted on panel
120 x 120 cm

ãir 1, S.: aria; apparenza, *f.;* aspetto, *m.;* cantata, *f.*, canto, *m.: in the open* —, all'aria aperta; *beat the* —, far un buco nell'acqua; *build castles in the* —, far castelli in aria; *take the* —, pigliar aria. **air** 2, TR.: mettere all'aria, sventolare; seccare. **-balloon,** S.: pallone aerostatico, *m.* **-bladder,** S.: vescica, *f.* **-built,** ADJ.: chimerico, vano. **-drawn,** ADJ.: finto, ideale. **-gun,** S.: fucile a vento, *m.* **-hole,** S.: sfogatoio; spiraglio, *m.* **-iness,** S.: esporre all'aria, *m.;* leggerezza, vivacità. **-ing,** S.: l'esporre all'aria, *m.;* aerazione, passeggiata, *f.* **-less,** ADJ.: senz'aria. **-pump,** S.: tromba pneumatica, *f.* **-shaft,** S.: spiraglio, *m.* **-y,** ADJ.: d'aria, aereo, giulivo

RICHARD SERRA
San Francisco, California 1939

Prop, 1968
2 elements
lead antimony,
sheet, 108,5 x 100 cm
rod, lenght 214 cm

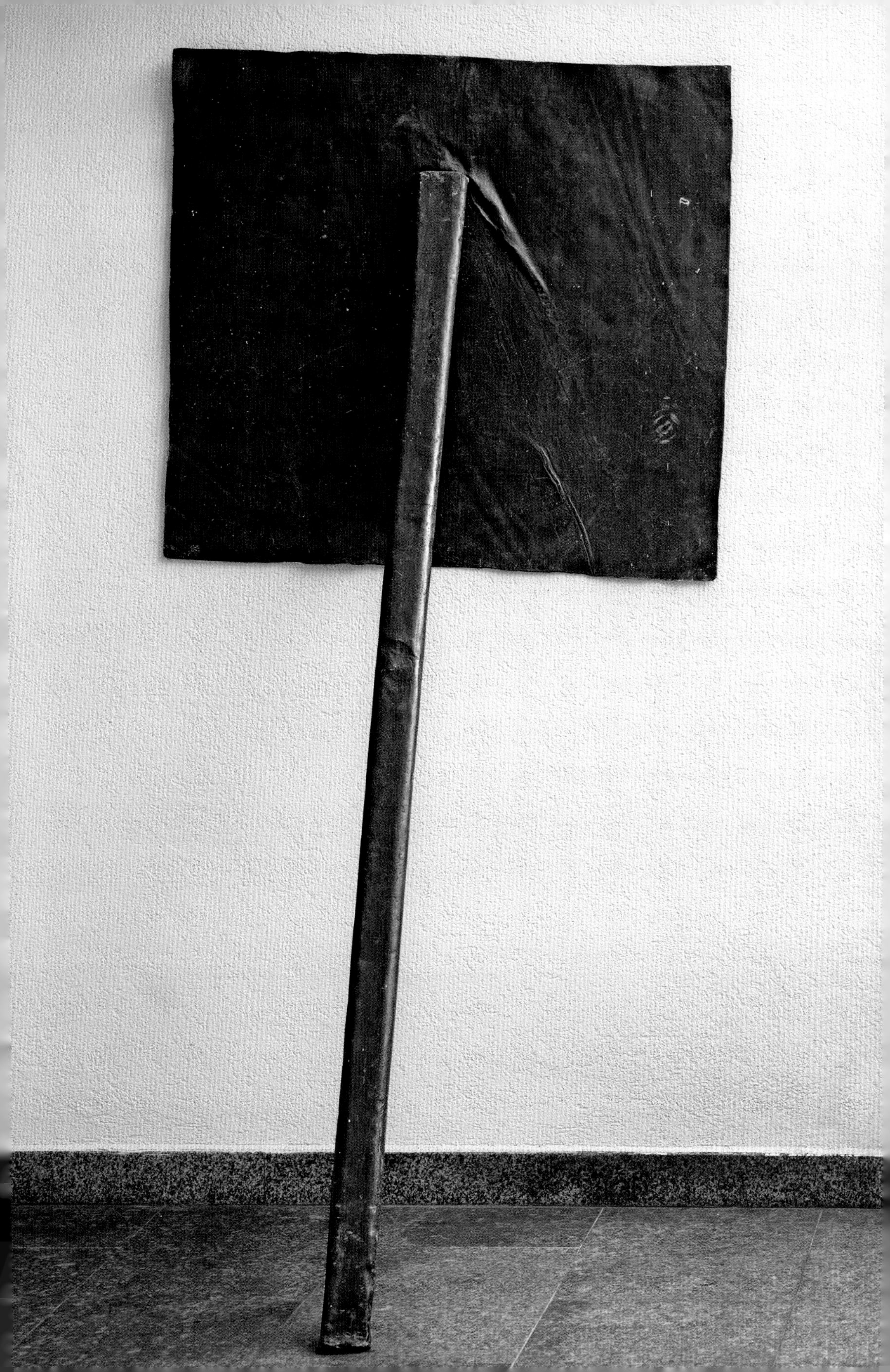

BRUCE NAUMAN
Fort Wayne, Indiana 1941

None Sing / Neon Sign,
1970
ruby-red and cool-
white neon
33 x 61,5 x 3,8 cm

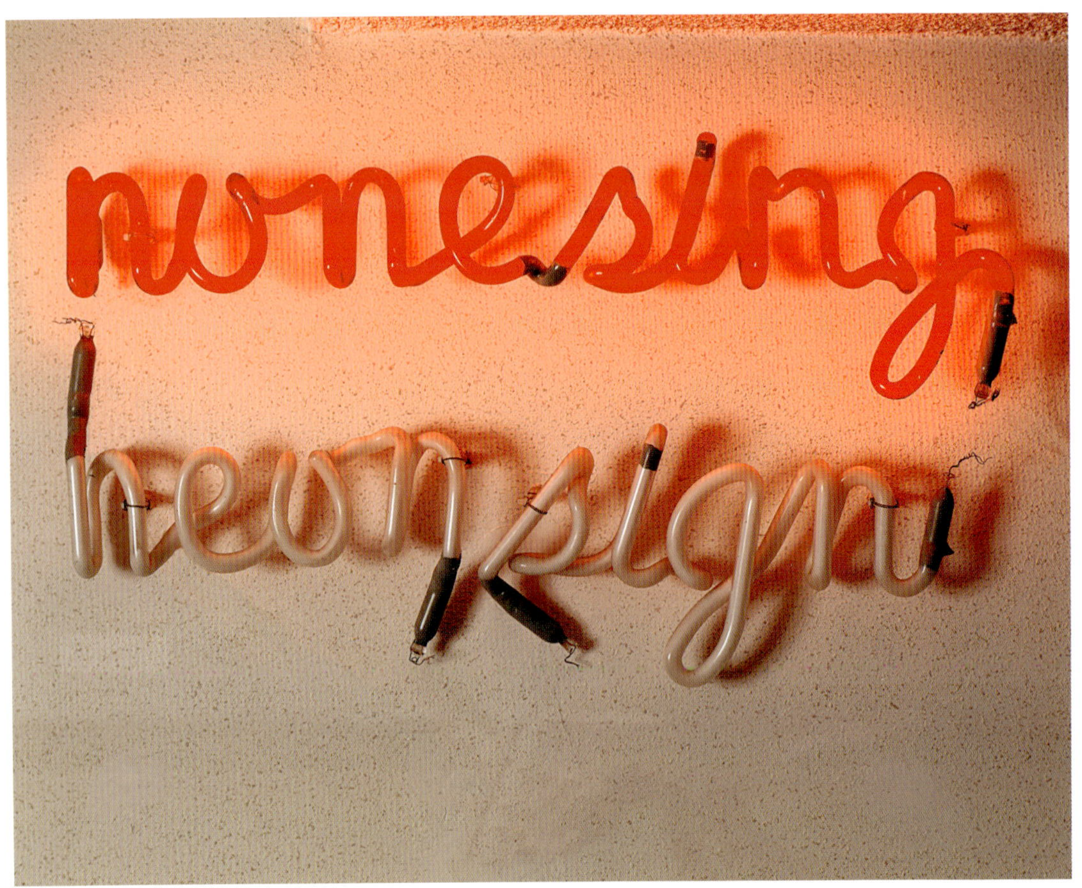

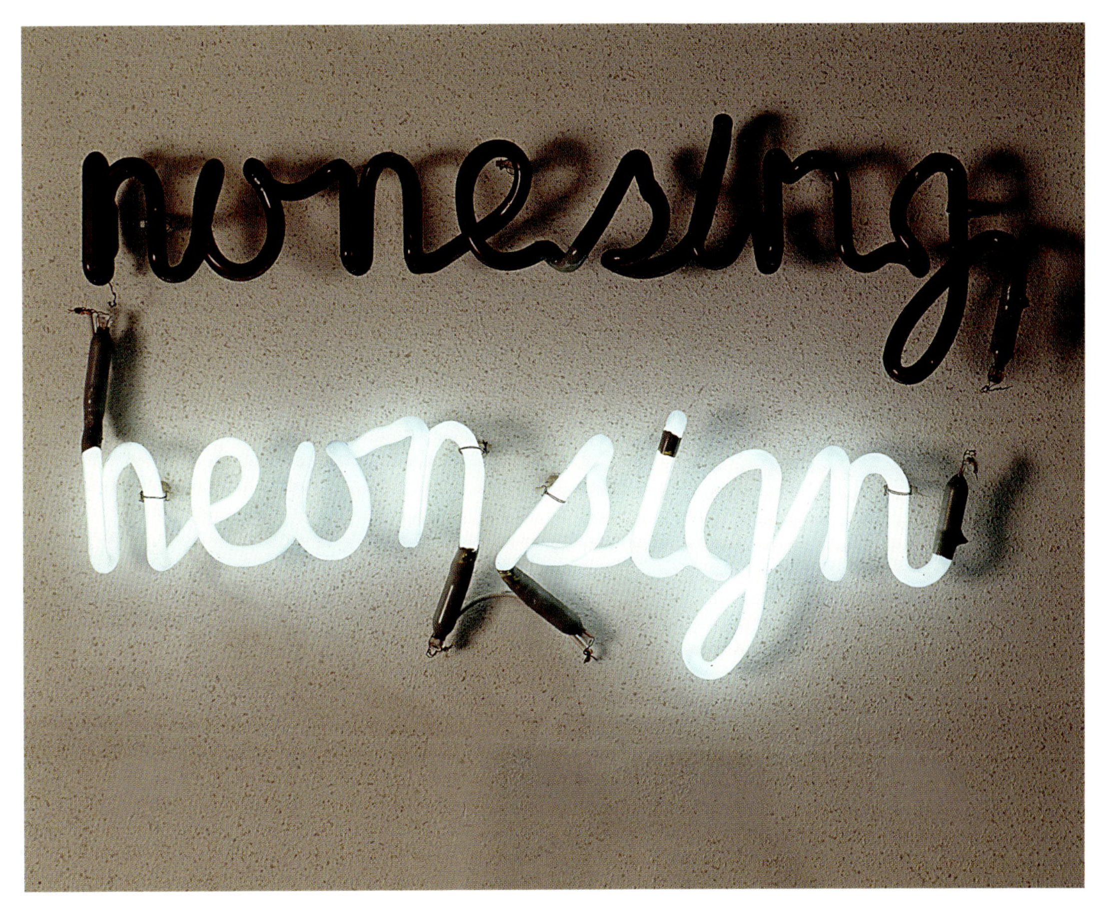
none sing
neon sign

MICHAEL HEIZER
Berkeley, California 1944

Sunset, 1969
colour slide, fiberglass
161,5 x 155,5 cm

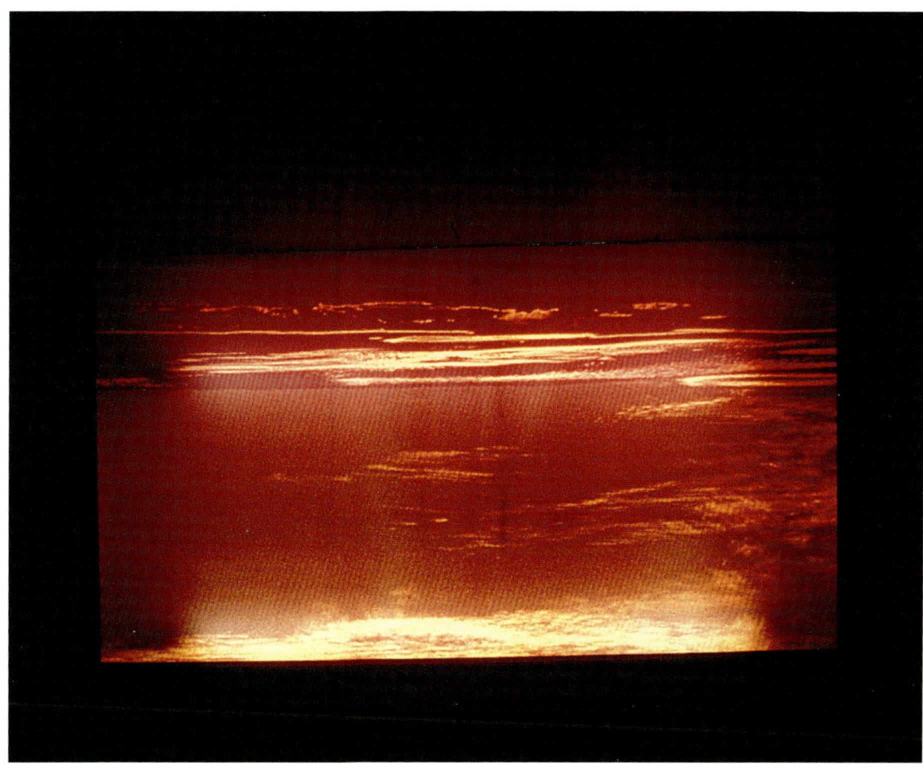

MICHAEL HEIZER
Berkeley, California 1944

Displaced Mass.
Art Before Life 5,
1968-1969
photograph, metal
sheet
115,5 x 91,5 cm

Art before Life 5

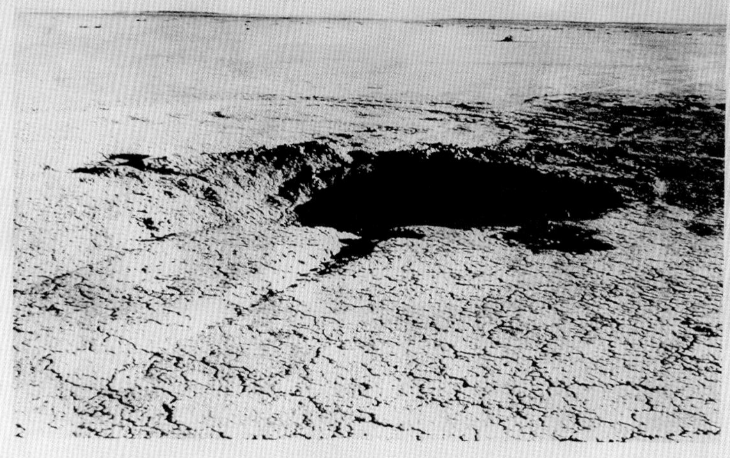

1/69

1/69 California 15' dia. mechanical, chemical

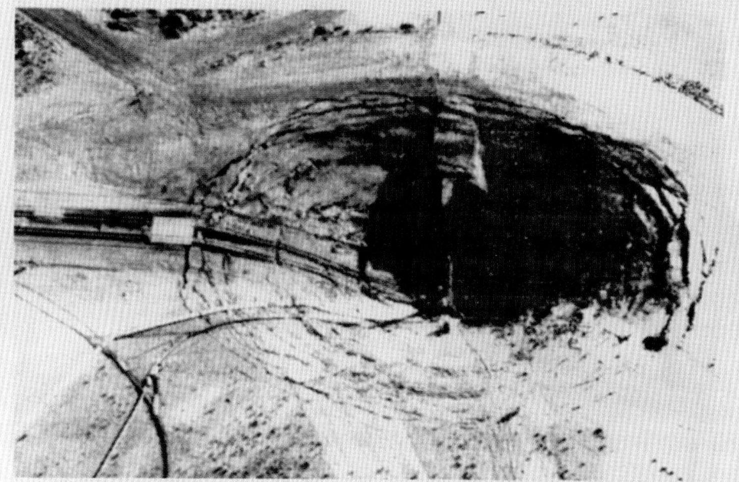

12/69

12/69 Nevada 350' dia. chemical

EDWARD RUSCHA
Omaha, Nebraska 1937

Two Sheets Stained with Ivy and Tobacco, 1973
gunpowder, ivy and tobacco stains on paper
58 x 73,5 cm

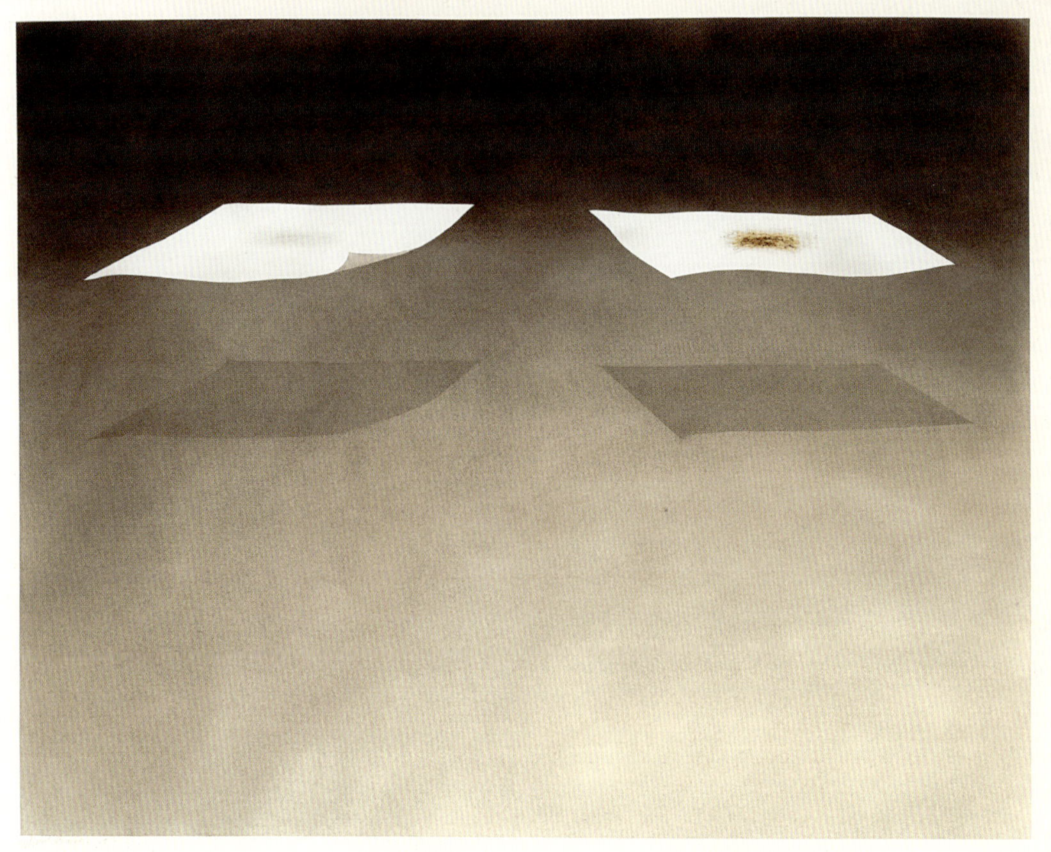

EDWARD RUSCHA
Omaha, Nebraska 1937

Suspended Sheet Stained with Blood, 1973
gunpowder, blood stain on paper
58 x 73,5 cm

on the following pages

DAN FLAVIN
Jamaica, New York 1933
- Riverhead, New York 1996

Untitled (to Giuseppe Agrati), 1968
yellow fluorescent lights
122 x 335 cm

IN THE SPRING OF 1963, I FELT SUFFICIENTLY FOUNDED IN MY NEW WORK TO DISCONTINUE IT.
I TOOK UP A RECENT DIAGRAM AND DECLARED "THE DIAGONAL OF A PERSONAL ECSTASY" (*THE DIAGONAL OF MAY*, 1963) TO BE AN ORDINARY EIGHT-FOOT FLUOURESCENT LIGHT FIXTURE, IN ALL COMMERCIALLY-AVAILABLE COLOURS. I CHOSE GOLD TO START WITH.
THE RADIANT TUBE AND THE SHADOW CAST BY ITS SUPPORTING PAN SEEMED IRONIC ENOUGH TO HOLD ALONE. THERE WAS LITERALLY NO NEED TO COMPOSE THIS SYSTEM DEFINITIVELY: IT SEEMED TO SUSTAIN ITSELF DIRECTLY, DYNAMICALLY, DRAMATICALLY ON MY WORKROOM WALL – A BUOYANT AND INSISTENT GASEOUS IMAGE WHICH, THROUGH BRILLIANCE, SOMEWHAT BETRAYED ITS PHYSICAL PRESENCE INTO APPROXIMATE INVISIBILITY.

DAN FLAVIN

"...in daylight or cool white". An Autobiographical Sketch, in "Artforum", v. IV, no. 4, New York, December 1965

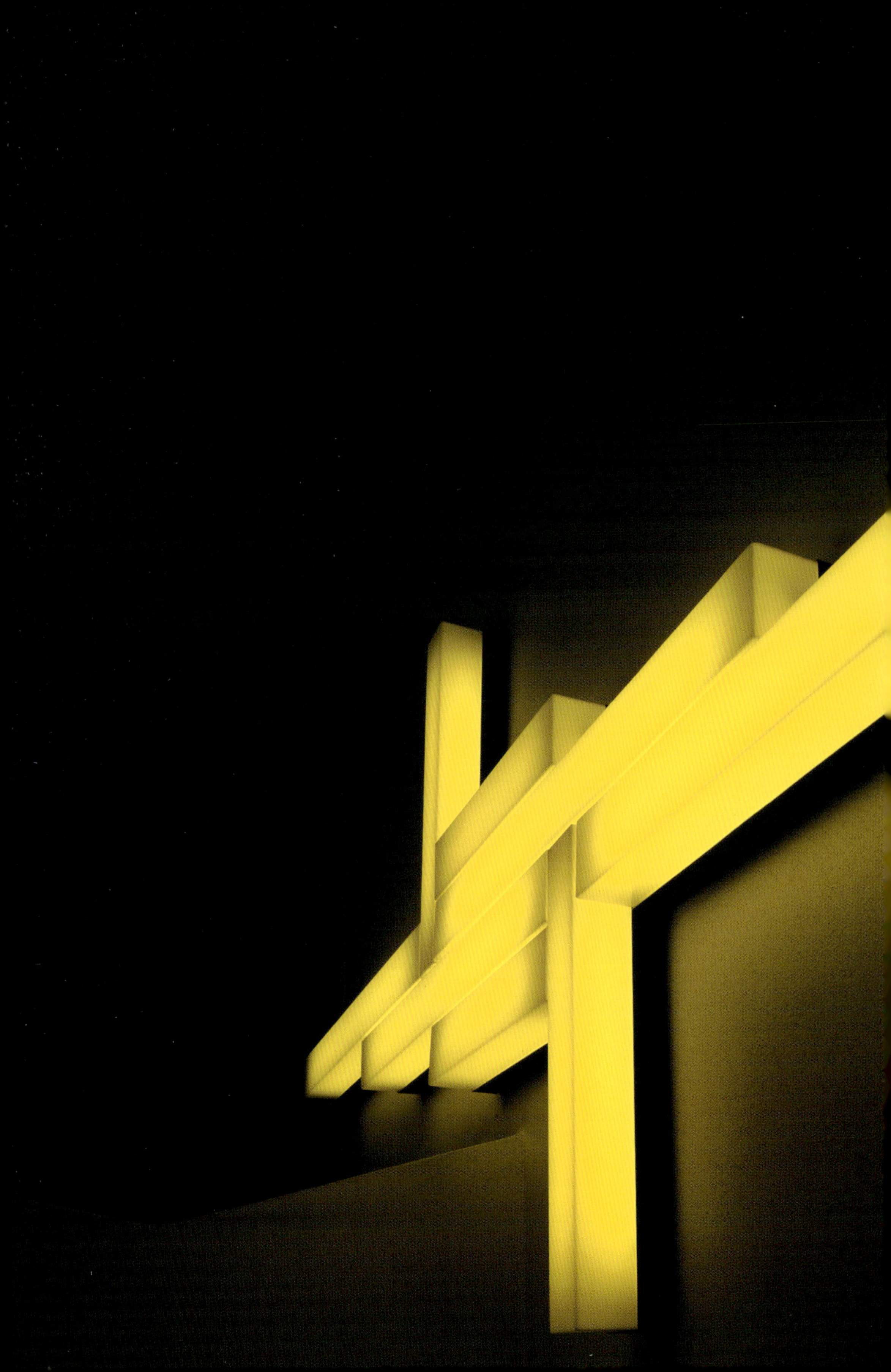

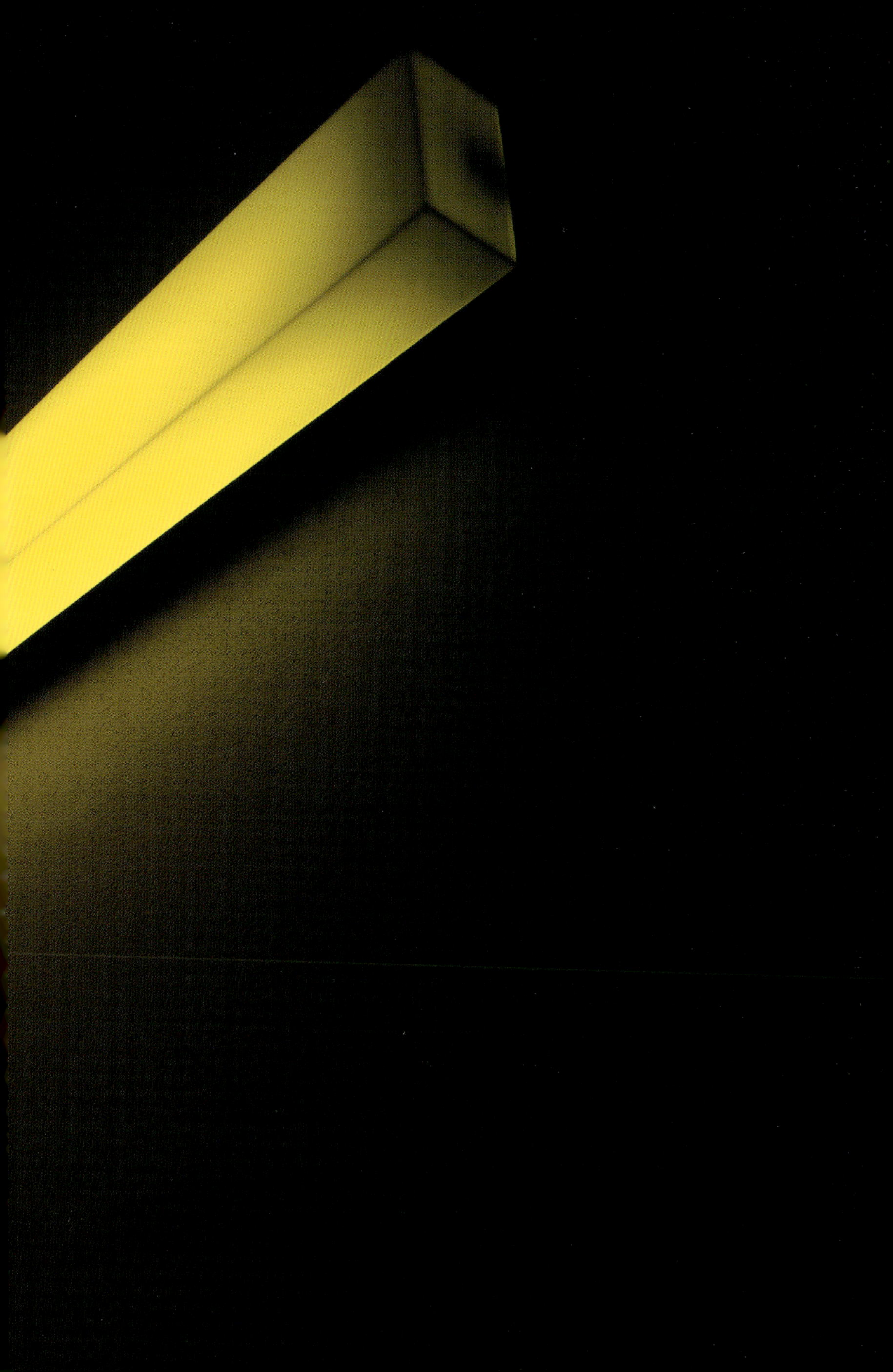

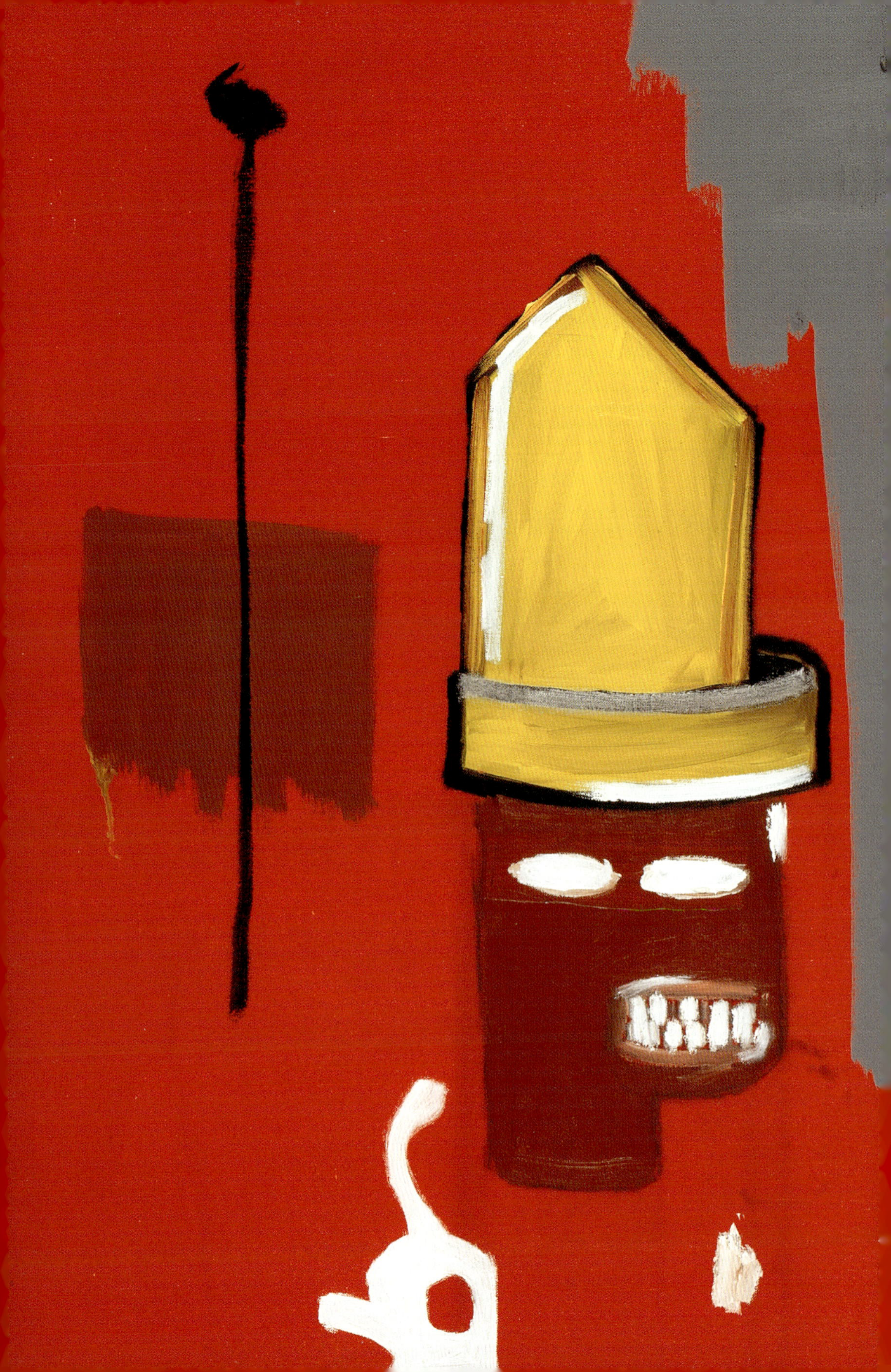

NEW ICONS
OF AMERICAN ART

IN 1963, ANDY WARHOL DEDICATED A SERIES OF WORKS TO A POPULAR ROCK ICON: ELVIS PRESLEY. WARHOL SOURCED THE IMAGE OF THE SINGER FROM A STILL FROM THE WESTERN FILM *FLAMING STAR* (1960), SILKSCREENING IT ONTO THE CANVAS IN THREE OVERLAPPING IMAGES. THANKS TO THE MULTIPLYING – TYPICAL OF MEANS OF MASS COMMUNICATION – AND OVERLAPPING OF THE IMAGE, THE FIGURE ALMOST APPEARS TO MOVE BACK AND FORTH AGAINST A NEUTRAL SILVER BACKGROUND. THIS WORK WAS PURCHASED, LIKE THE OTHERS IN THE LUIGI AND PEPPINO AGRATI COLLECTION, FROM THE PRESTIGIOUS CASTELLI GALLERY IN NEW YORK.

ANDY WARHOL
Pittsburgh, Pennsylvania 1928 – New York 1987

Triple Elvis, 1963
acrylic and silkscreen on canvas
208 x 152 cm

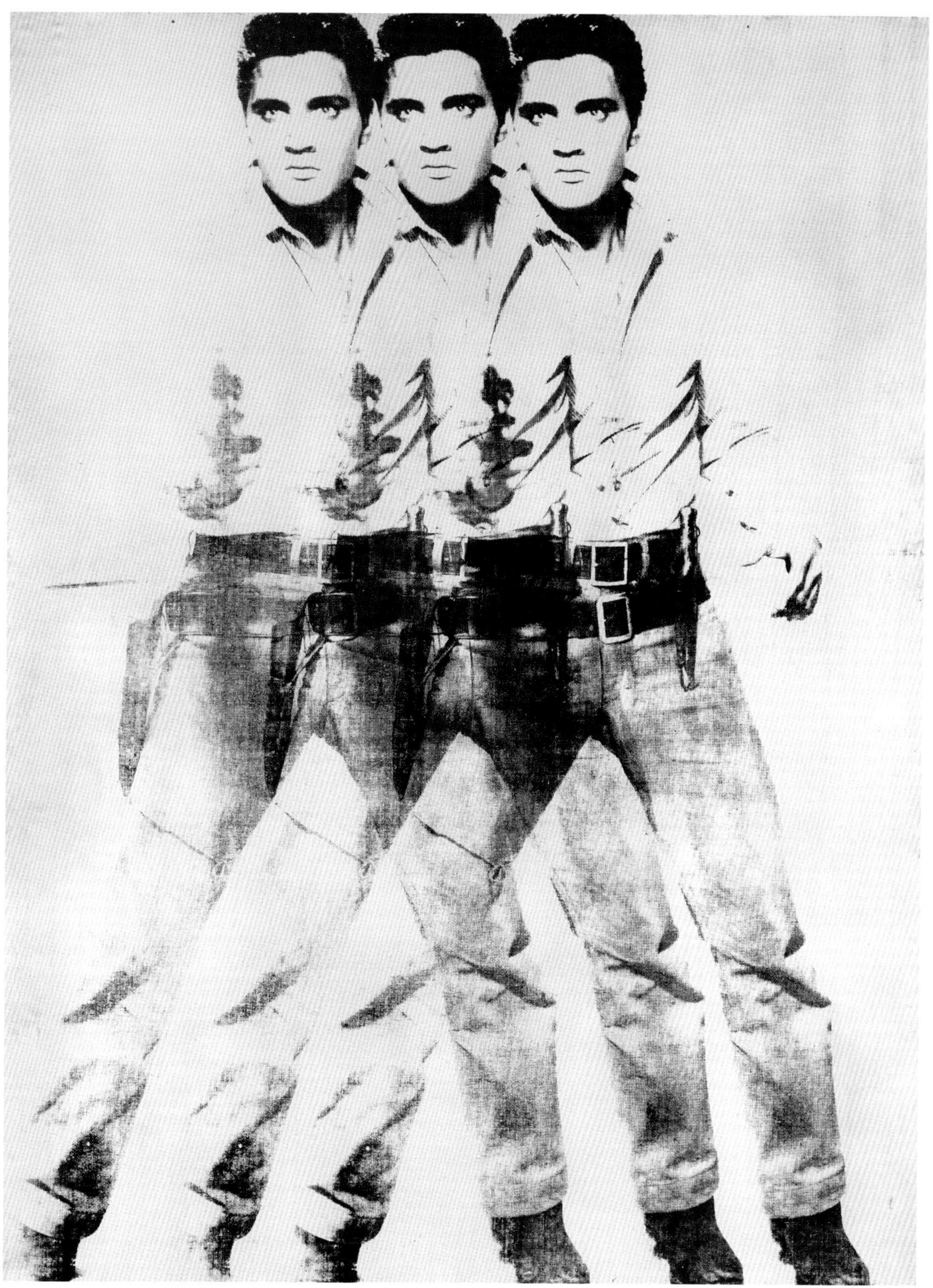

ROBERT
RAUSCHENBERG
Port Arthur, Texas 1925
- Captiva, Florida 2008

Blue Exit, 1961
oil, graphite on
canvas
213,5 x 153,5 cm

on the following pages

ROBERT
RAUSCHENBERG
Port Arthur, Texas 1925
- Captiva, Florida 2008

Untitled (Scripture III),
1974
rope, cans, black
pencil, acrylic, gauze,
newspaper photos
transferred onto
paper
215 x 150 cm

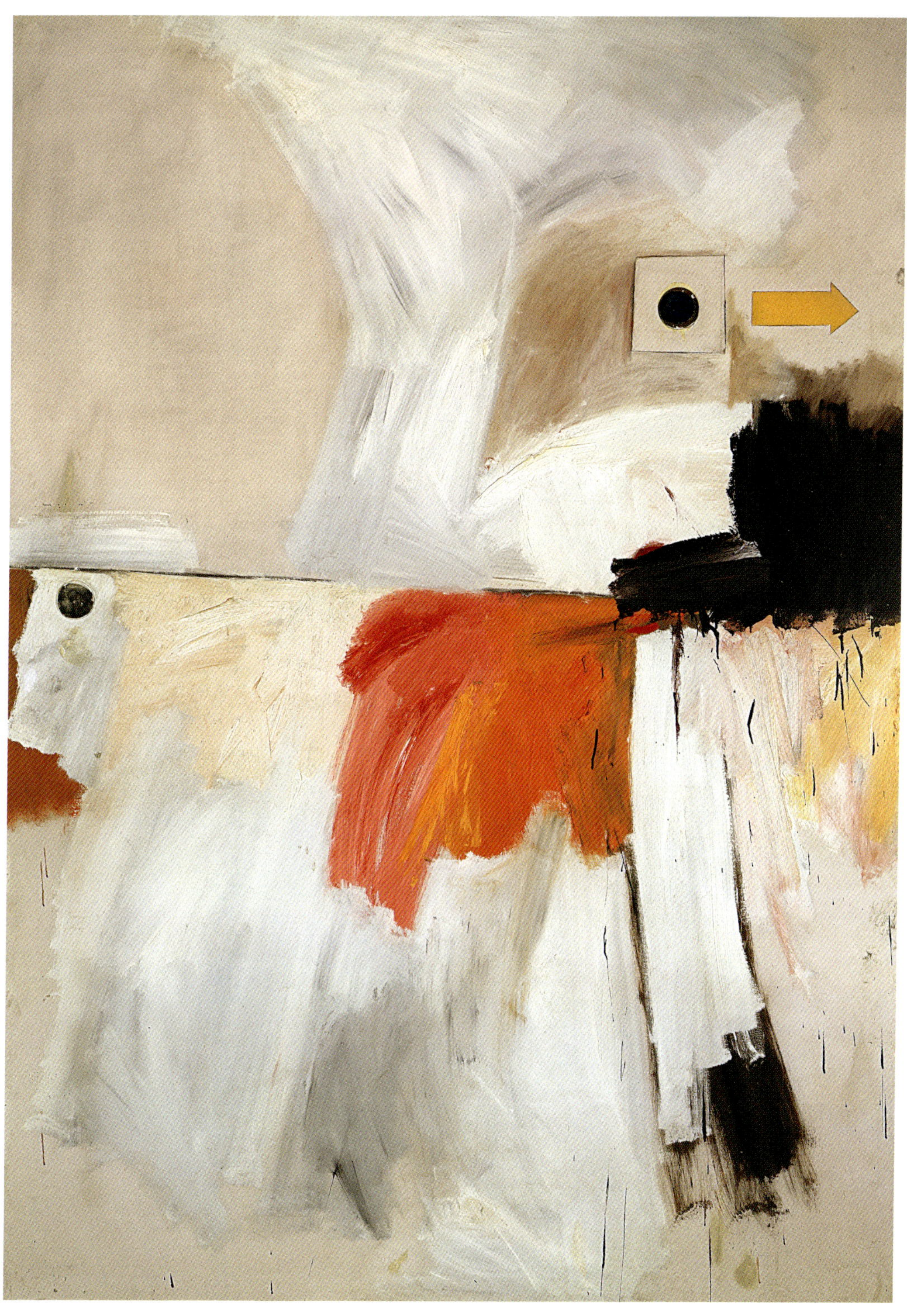

WHAT DO YOU CALL WHAT YOU MAKE?
I CALL THEM *COMBINE-PAINTINGS* – THAT IS, COMBINED WORKS, COMBINATIONS. IT'S A WAY FOR ME TO AVOID CATEGORIES. IF I HAD CALLED MY WORKS PAINTINGS, PEOPLE WOULD HAVE SAID THEY WERE SCULPTURES; IF I HAD CALLED THEM SCULPTURES, THEY WOULD HAVE BEEN DESCRIBED AS BAS-RELIEFS OR PAINTINGS.

WHY DO YOU INCLUDE BOTTLES, STRINGS, CHAIRS AND VARIOUS OBJECTS IN YOUR WORKS, YOUR COMBINE-PAINTINGS?
I DON'T HAVE A SPECIFIC AIM. THE COLOURS USED BY PAINTERS ARE ALSO MANUFACTURED OBJECTS. I WISH TO INCORPORATE ANY OBJECT LINKED TO EVERYDAY LIFE INTO MY CANVAS.

IS IT A POETIC ATTEMPT?
IT'S TOPICALITY. [...]

COULDN'T WE DESCRIBE YOUR PAINTING – DUE TO THE WAY YOU USE, EXTOL, EXALT THESE OBJECTS – AS INSPIRED BY A SORT OF WASTE AESTHETIC?
IN A WAY. PARADOXICALLY, HOWEVER, THESE MATERIALS CEASE TO BE WASTE ONCE THEY'VE BEEN REUSED.

ROBERT RAUSCHENBERG

Interview with Robert Rauschenberg by André Parinaud, in "Arts", no. 821, Paris, 1-16 May 1961

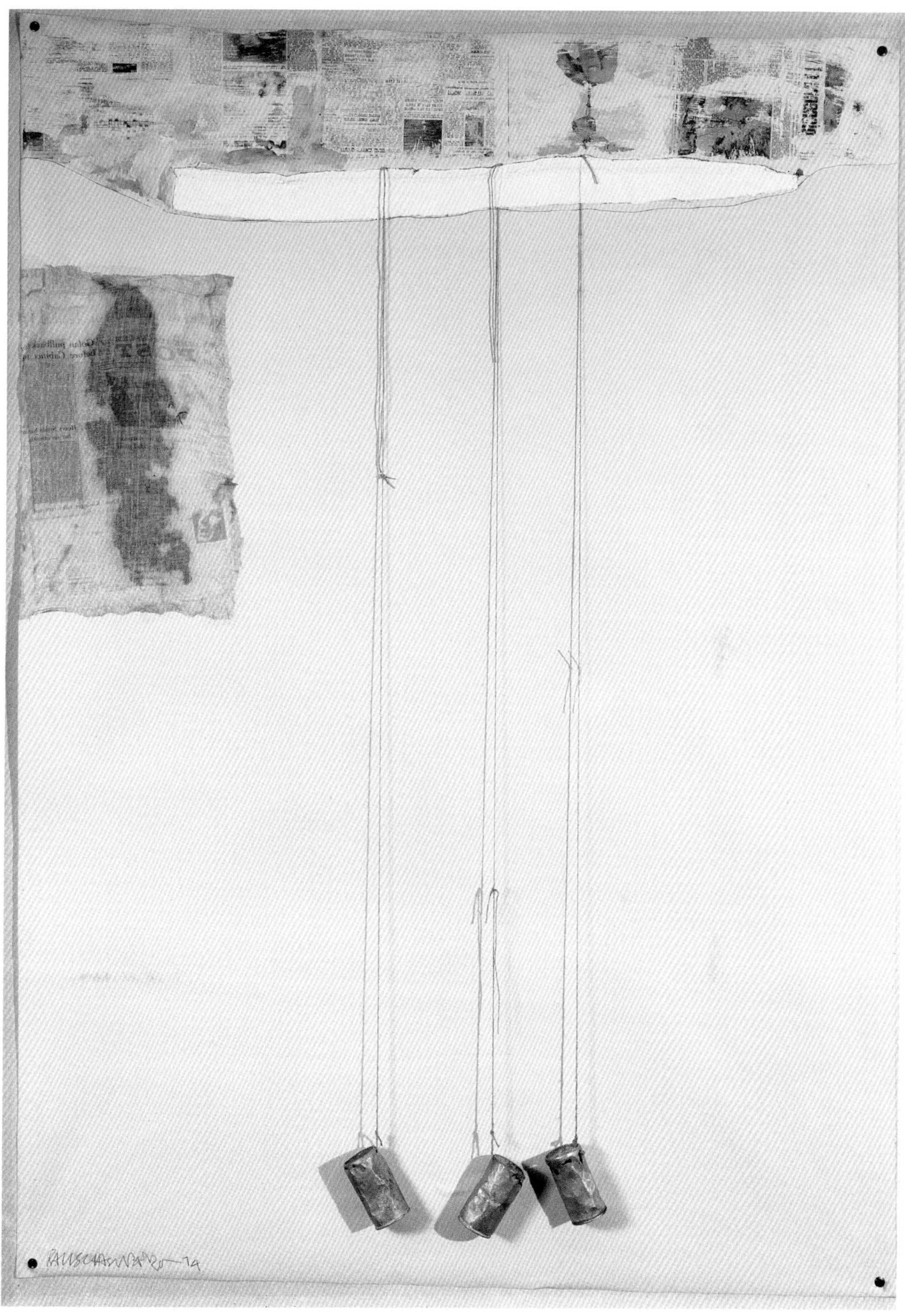

ROBERT
RAUSCHENBERG
Port Arthur, Texas 1925
- Captiva, Florida 2008

Trasmettitore Argento Glut (Neapolitan) [Silver Transmitter Glut (Neapolitan)],
1987
metal and number plate assemblage
249 x 320 x 32 cm

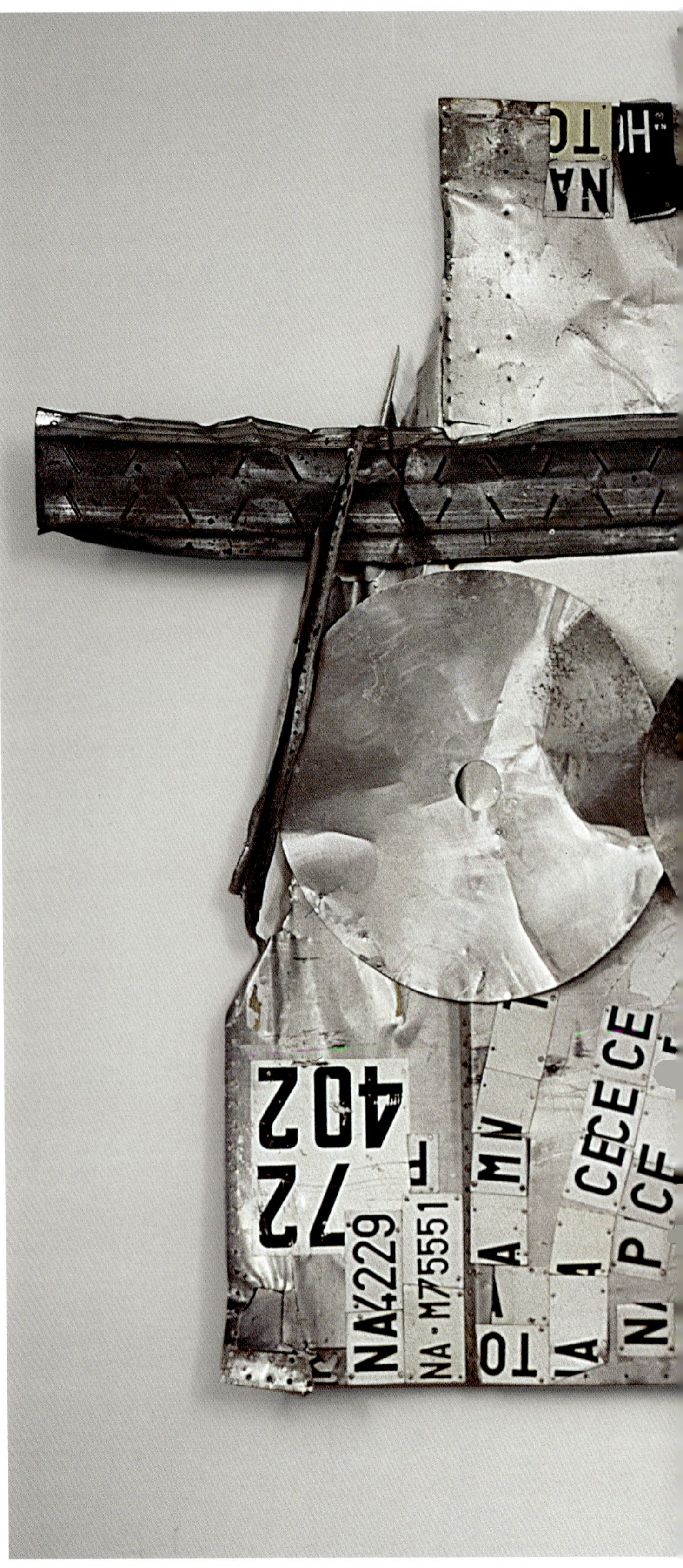

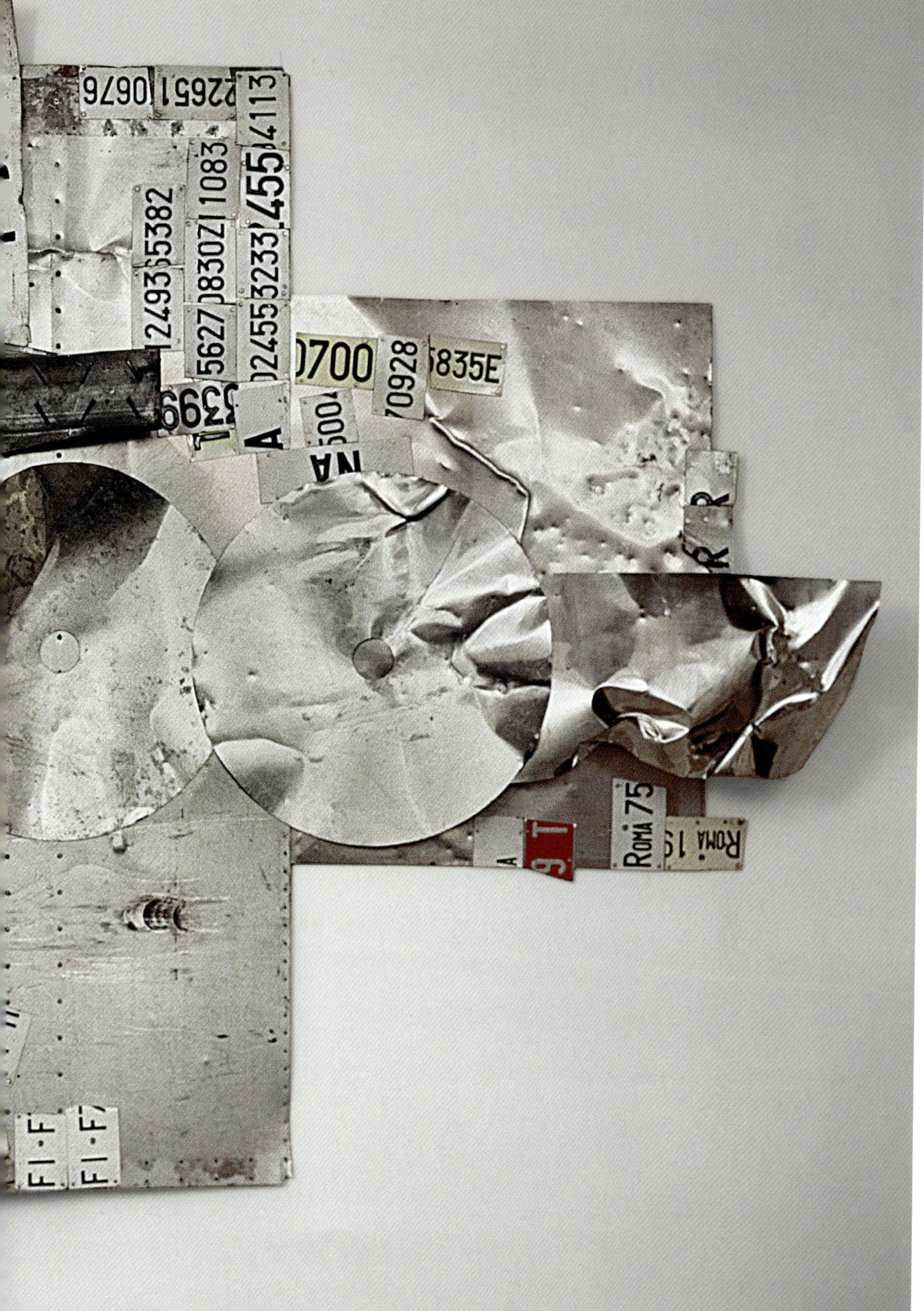

CY TWOMBLY
Lexington, Virginia 1929
- Rome 2011

Diana Passes, 1962
oil, crayon and pencil
on canvas
130 x 150 cm

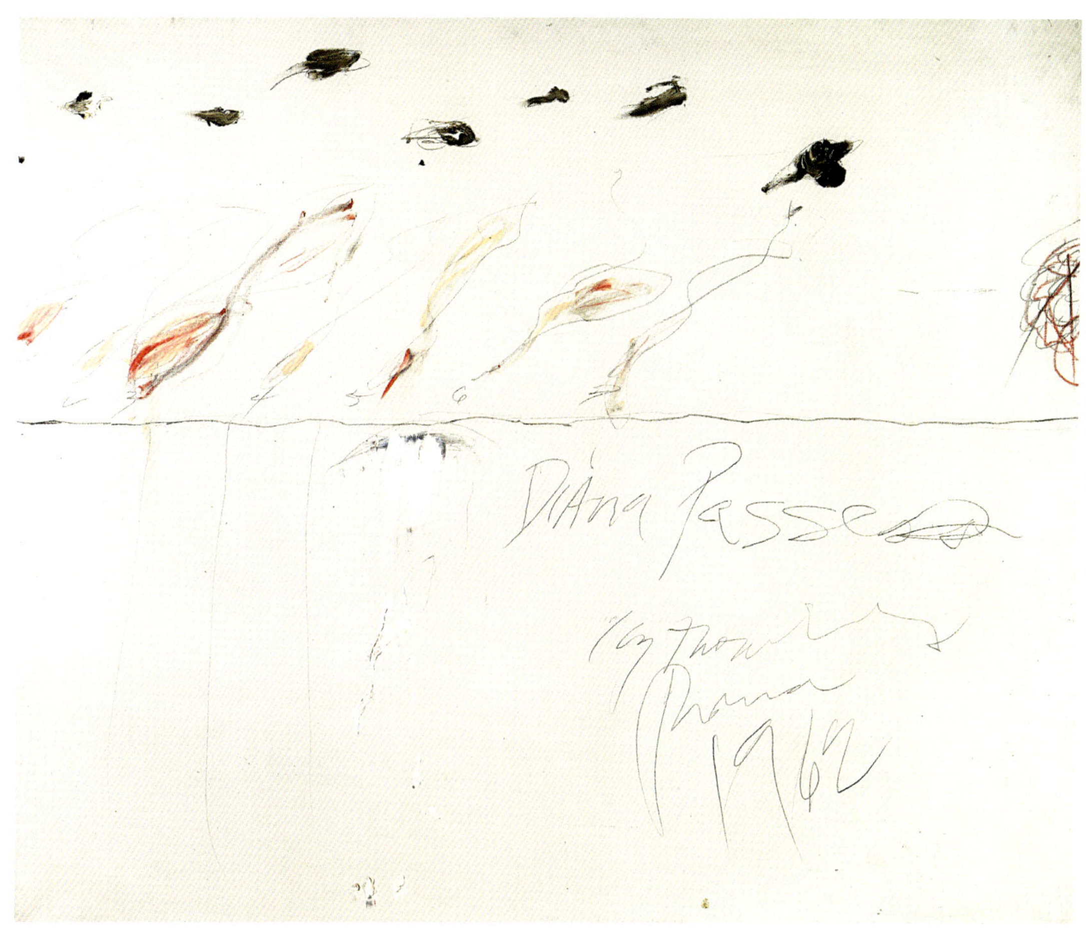

CY TWOMBLY
Lexington, Virginia 1929
- Rome 2011

Untitled, 1966
cementite, pencil,
crayon on canvas
190 x 200 cm

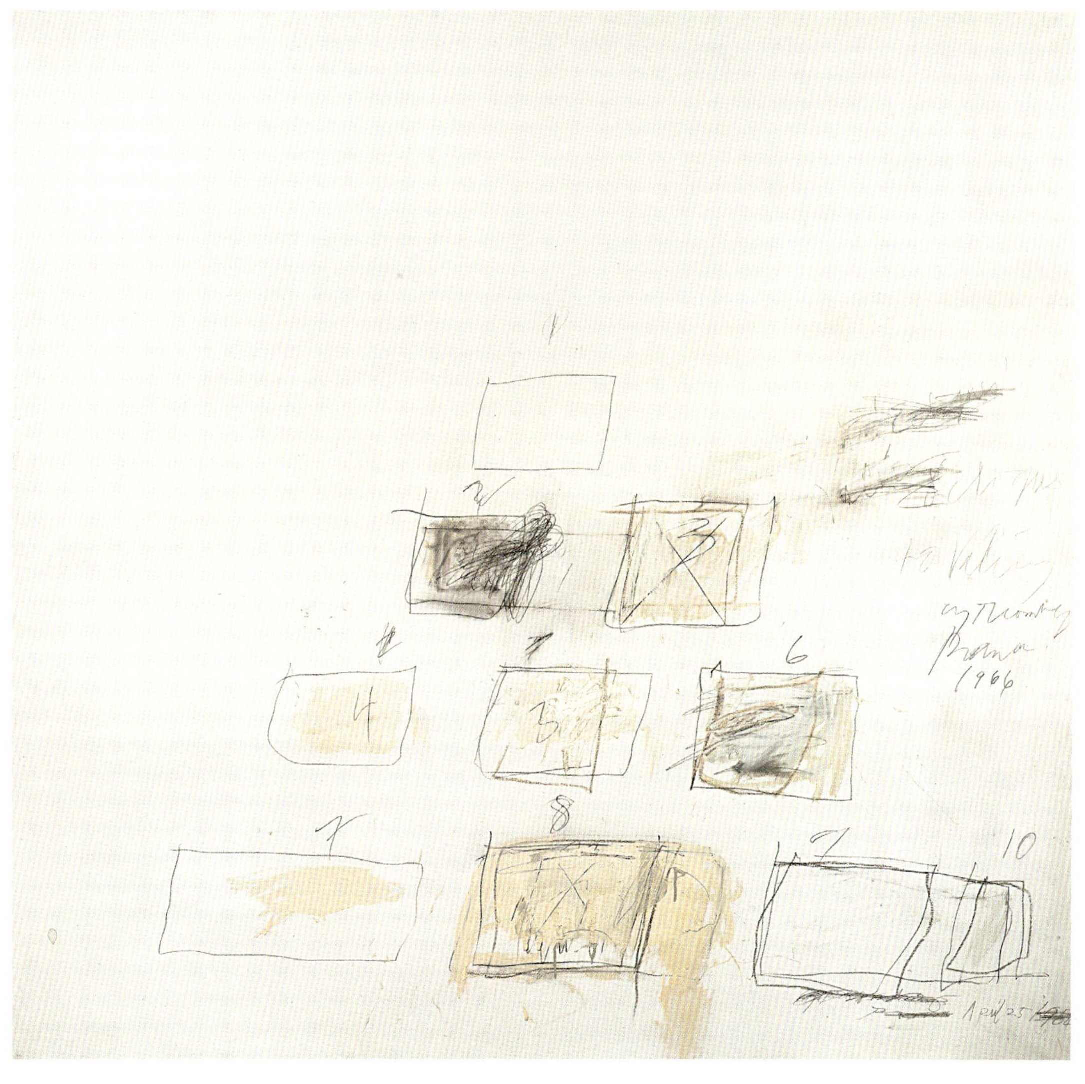

JEAN-MICHEL
BASQUIAT
Brooklyn, New York 1960
- New York 1988

Financial District, 1985
acrylic, oil on canvas
163 x 142 cm

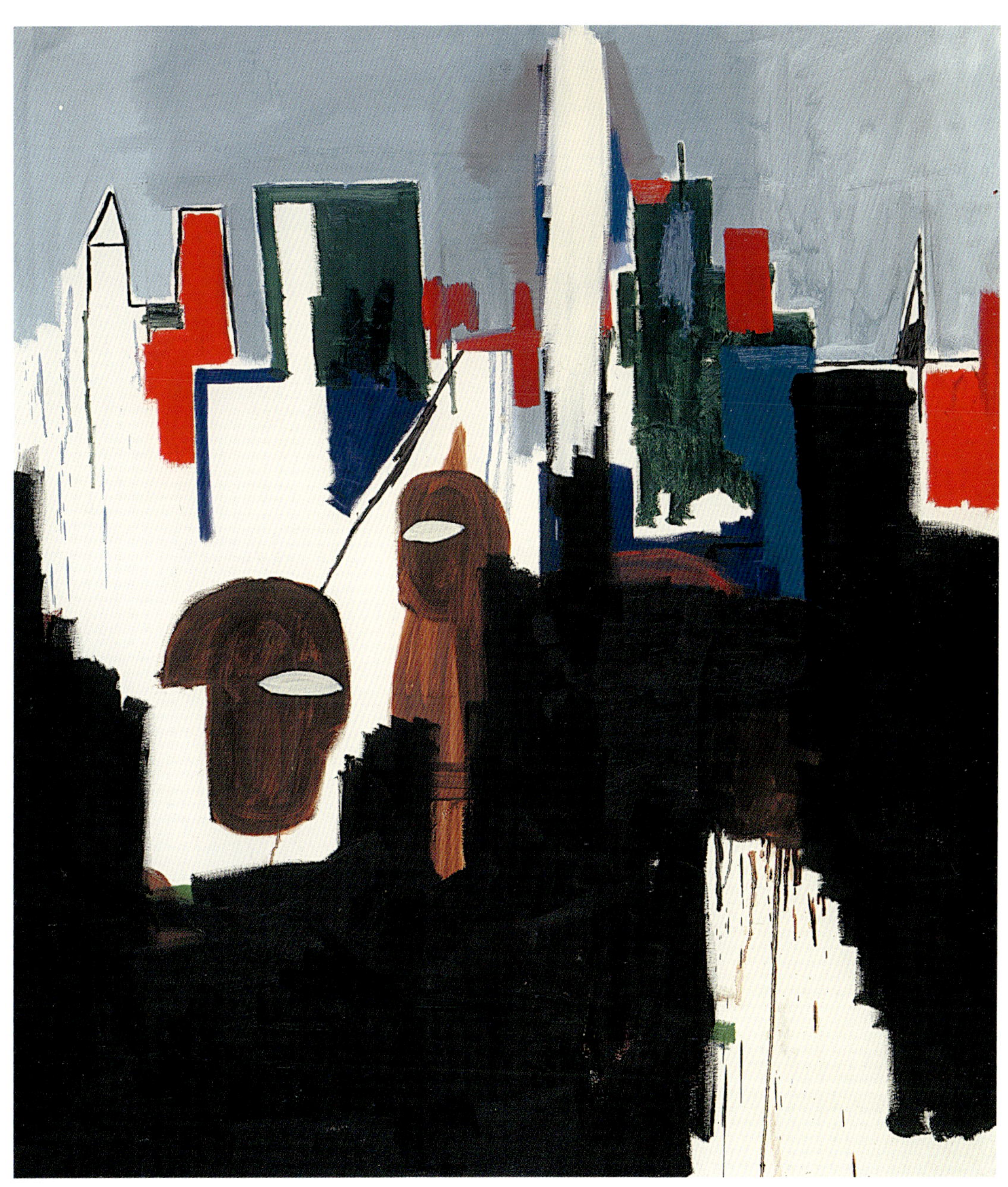

JEAN-MICHEL
BASQUIAT
Brooklyn, New York 1960
- New York 1988

Alchemist, 1986
oil, gold paint on
canvas
126 x 100 cm

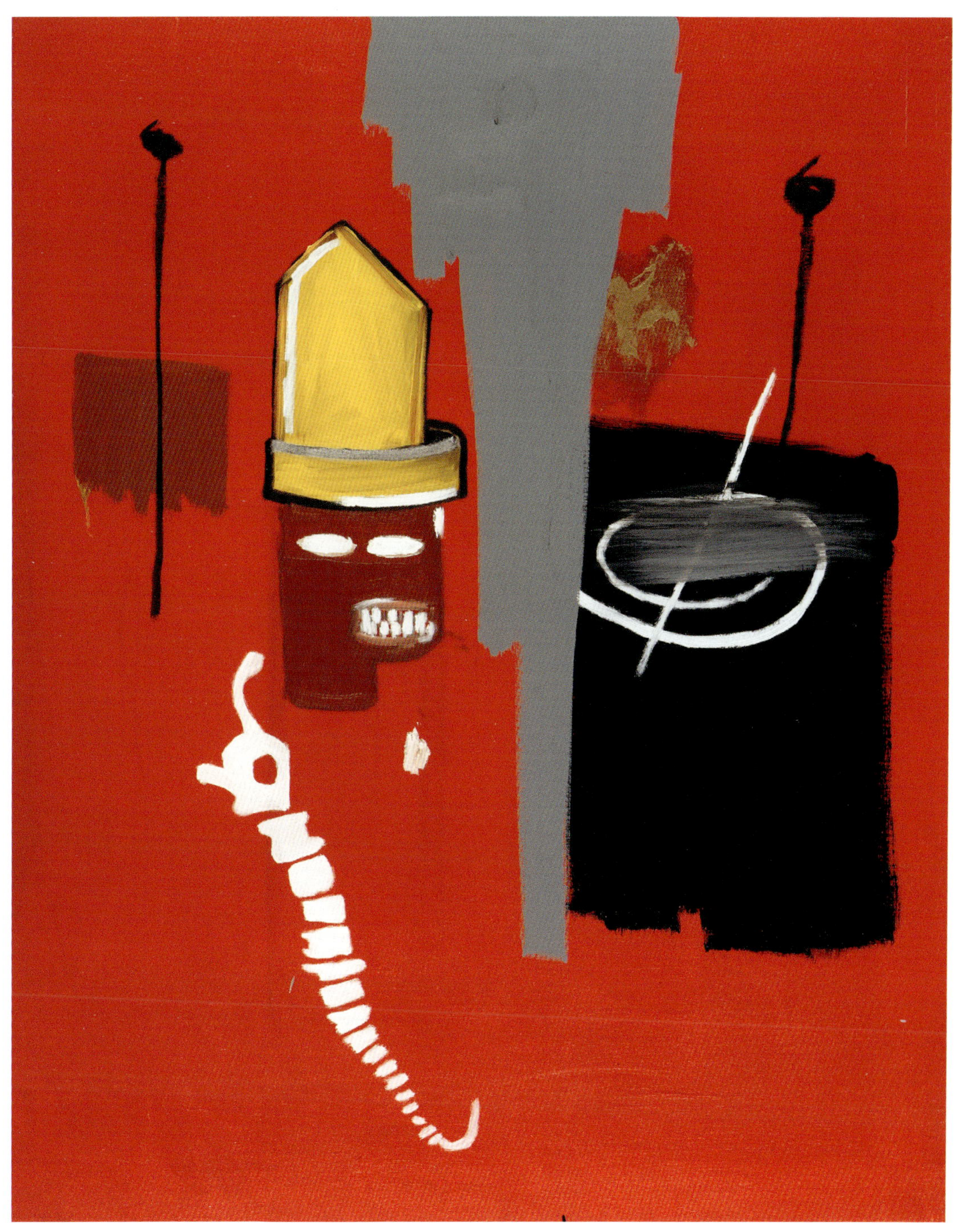

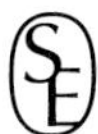

Silvana Editoriale

Direction
Dario Cimorelli

Art Director
Giacomo Merli

Editorial Coordinator
Sergio Di Stefano

Copy Editor
Lorena Ansani

Layout
Denise Castelnovo

Production Coordinator
Antonio Micelli

Editorial Assistant
Ondina Granato

Photo Editor
Alessandra Olivari, Silvia Sala

Press Office
Lidia Masolini, press@silvanaeditoriale.it

Cover
Christo (Christo Javacheff)
Wrapped Monument to Vittorio Emanuele (Project for Piazza del Duomo, Milan), 1970, detail

Photo credits
Luca Carrà, Milan
Giorgio Colombo, Milan
Antonia Mulas, Milan
Emilio Negri, Casatenovo
Vaglia-Luisi, Milan

Silvana Editoriale S.p.A.
via dei Lavoratori, 78
20092 Cinisello Balsamo, Milan
tel. 02 453 951 01
fax 02 453 951 51
www.silvanaeditoriale.it

Reproductions, printing
and binding in Italy
Printed by Tipo Stampa s.r.l.,
Moncalieri (Turin)
Printed May 2018